ENGLAN

Richard Ingrams was founder and editor of *Private Eye*. Apart from the Private Eye books, he is author of *Piper's Places: John Piper in England and Wales* (1983), *God's Apology: A Chronicle of Three Friends* (1986) and *John Stewart Collis: A Memoir* (1987).

ENGLAND

An Anthology

COMPILED BY
RICHARD INGRAMS

WITH WOOD ENGRAVINGS BY
JOHN O'CONNOR

Fontana
An Imprint of HarperCollins*Publishers*

First published in Great Britain in 1990 by Collins

This edition first issued in 1991 by Fontana,
an imprint of HarperCollins Publishers,
77/85 Fulham Palace Road,
Hammersmith, London W6 8JB

9 8 7 6 5 4 3 2 1

Set in Itek Meridien by
Ace Filmsetting Ltd, Frome, Somerset
Printed and bound by
HarperCollins Book Manufacturing, Glasgow

CONTENTS

England, with all thy faults, I love thee still –
My country! and, while yet a nook is left
Where English minds and manners may be found,
Shall be constrain'd to love thee. Though thy clime
Be fickle, and thy year must part deform'd
With dripping rains, or wither'd by a frost,
I would not yet exchange thy sullen skies,
And fields without a flow'r, for warmer France
With all her vines; nor for Ausonia's groves
Of golden fruitage, and her myrtle bow'rs.

WILLIAM COWPER, from 'The Task'

Blind, tormented, unwearied, marvellous England.

JOHN RUSKIN

INTRODUCTION

Like everything else, it's been done before. There is nothing new in the idea of an anthology about England. On the other hand I can plead there is not much that is particularly English about those previous efforts. Most of them date from either the First or the Second World War when politicians, publishers and patriotic poets felt the need to encapsulate in prose and poetry the English heritage that we were supposed to be fighting for. The anthologists were unashamed flag-waggers and they all tended to include the same items – John O'Gaunt's speech, Rupert Brooke's 'Soldier', Wordsworth's sonnet 'Upon Westminster Bridge'.

There is nothing wrong with such pieces, apart from the fact that they are not really about England at all. Rupert Brooke's famous sonnet would be equally effective as a poem if one were to substitute, say, Finland for England throughout; and Robert Browning for that matter might just as well have wished to be in Greenville, Mississippi 'Now that April's there'.

When I first set to work on this anthology I felt uncomfortable about the irrelevance of much of the literature of the past. This was not just a question of the sentiments expressed by the likes of Rupert Brooke. Even the topography had changed. No one, to take an obvious example, can today stand on Westminster Bridge and exclaim with Wordsworth that 'Earth has not anything to show more fair'. The desecration of the view of St Paul's Cathedral, a symbol of England which has cropped up again and again, sometimes in the most unexpected places, typifies the general desecration that has been taking place over the last fifty years or so, leaving the country covered with motorways and pylons, hideous urban developments and all the ugly debris of the twentieth century.

But it was precisely this feeling of mine about present-day

England that gave me my cue. The more I read the more I realized how my own lukewarm indignation about the vandalism perpetrated by my generation was itself a traditional English emotion. In fact it was altogether more representative of the authentic English spirit than the slightly bogus patriotism of the flag-waggers like Rupert Brooke. I discovered, if I did not know it already, that running through the whole of our literature, especially that of the Romantic era and beyond, is a deeply held conviction on the part of the nobler spirits that the country is irrevocably doomed. One could almost compile a whole anthology on this theme, entitled *Going to the Dogs*. Here I will quote only one example, from the index to the 1892 two-volume edition of Dr Johnson's letters:

> ENGLAND, all trade dead II 120; poverty and degradation, 150; sinking, 264; fear of a civil war, 286; times dismal and gloomy, 370; see also INVASIONS.

(In passing it is worth saying how appropriate it should be that Dr Johnson is still regarded as the quintessential Englishman, a man whose popular image is that of a convivial old party seated in a tavern surrounded by cronies, but who was in private a deeply melancholy man troubled by all kinds of doubts and feelings of guilt. If anyone in our own day corresponds to that persona it is the late Poet Laureate John Betjeman, another very English Englishman who, behind his jolly, avuncular façade, was inwardly tormented.)

Melancholy and nostalgia are abiding characteristics of the English. Cricket is our national game but the most famous line of cricketing literature (unintelligible to any foreigner) – 'Oh my Hornby and my Barlow long ago' – typically harks back to the cricket matches of the past and the very English names of two totally forgotten men. It strikes a chord. Dickens strikes a chord arguably more than anyone because he describes a never-never England of crowded inns, foggy alleyways and cosy firesides, an England just out of reach which we all long to recapture, like a fading dream, but which we know never existed in reality. Of all the elements in the Dickensian dream-world perhaps the most vivid is the idea of home as the ideal towards which all our efforts are directed. Foreigners, as you will see, tend to mock the sentimental English for hankering after their Home Sweet Home, but for the Englishman like me there is no more powerful passage in this book than that in which Kenneth Grahame describes the journey of Ratty and Mole through the December snow and the sudden and desperate longing to get home that assails poor Mole.

I first became aware of that kind of urge when I was sent to the Far East during my National Service in 1956. I remember gazing at pictures of English trees and green fields with an intensity as powerful as any pin-up might inspire. A few years later, after I had married, we set up home in an English village – unspoiled, it goes without saying – and it was then that I became aware not just of the seasons and the landscape, the birds and the wild flowers, but of all those writers who had described them with such passion and exactness, writers of whose existence I had not previously known because they are considered a minority taste and are consequently excluded from the school syllabus: Gilbert White, Dorothy Wordsworth, Francis Kilvert, Richard Jefferies. It was an anthology called *The English Year* by Geoffrey Grigson which first introduced me to them and I have remained grateful to Grigson ever since. He made me conscious of the mystical response to nature which runs through a great deal of our finest literature and which is generally overlooked by foreigners as they observe condescendingly the prosaic and philistine Englishman with his incomprehensible cricket and his inedible food.

There have been a great many such visitors over the centuries and they are well represented here. In the last century it seems to have been almost *de rigueur* for great men in America or on the Continent to visit England and record their impressions in writing. They were struck especially by London – its vastness, noise and squalor. They made due note of the famous fog, the black sooty buildings, the interminable dinners, the dismal Sunday afternoons. Everyone commented with amazement on the fact that the streets were crowded with young prostitutes. Progressive people might point to their absence today as a sign of the advances we have made, but the scenes described by Dostoyevsky and others won't go away so easily. The English brutality and coarseness of which those 'fallen women' were a living emblem are still with us and anyone with half an imagination can easily conjure up their ghosts today in Piccadilly or the Haymarket. In much the same way, although we may pride ourselves on the abolition of the death penalty the hangman is still a potent figure in the public imagination and the majority of Englishmen continue to support the restoration of the gallows.

So, while on the surface everything has changed, nothing has really changed at all. We still have our unique and unpredictable climate, believed by so many to be responsible for the national character; and in spite of what you read there is still a great deal of countryside left. (It is the towns which in some cases have changed out of all recognition.) The traditional English sports of football, cricket and bell-ringing noted by a French visitor in 1725 (p. 145) are as popular now as they were then, even if we no longer throw dead cats and dogs at passers-by – another favourite pastime, according to the same observer. Perhaps the whole fun of any anthology such as this is to draw attention to these examples of consistency and to reassure ourselves that we remain much as we always have been. All it amounts to is that the past can never be discounted. However many city centres are redeveloped, however many fields are built over, it is with us whether we like it or not. And the best writing takes it always into account. One of the most attractive English habits is that of going on 'outings' – jaunts round the countryside, visiting churches and cathedrals, villages and gardens – a fact which partly explains the continuing popularity of a book like Cobbett's *Rural Rides*. Cobbett was typically English not only in his travelling habits and his indignation about the way things were going but in his concern with history. He looked back rather than forward, like all the best Romantics. Each parish church was to him a reminder that things had once been otherwise and that there had 'passed away a glory from the earth'. He was one of those prophets who inspired a whole generation without being given any real credit for it. The great Victorians – Ruskin, the Carlyles, William Morris – all followed in his footsteps, all echoing his anger and his fierce patriotism.

I was surprised in compiling this book how often Ruskin thrust himself to the fore. He is today a neglected writer through no fault but his own: he wrote so much twaddle that anyone who embarks on one of his books will soon find himself bogged down. In an anthology one can extract out of the morass of lunatic speculation those passages which, besides being some of the best prose ever written, do reflect his intense love of the English landscape and the English past. Again one finds that English note of triumphant pessimism – London is irretrievably ruined by gerry-building, materialism has run rampant, even the climate is deteriorating and summer will soon cease to exist.

'Blind, tormented, unwearied, marvellous England.' I have used Ruskin's powerful phrase as an epigraph because if the extracts which follow have any kind of common thread it is that of damning and loving England in the same breath, so much so that one can sometimes trick oneself into believing that many of them have been written by the same hand, even though they may be separated by a hundred years or more.

When I started compiling this anthology I assumed that I would have to rely on all my friends for help. I have been surprised to find, despite the many promises made, how few suggestions have been forthcoming. I charitably put this down not to idleness on the part of my friends but more to a feeling they may have that an anthology ought to be a purely personal affair, and that therefore they have not liked to intrude. In the end the bulk of the extracts has come from my own books. Even so I would like to thank that great institution, the London Library, without which I could not have embarked on the project at all. I would also like to thank the faithful few who *did* rally round: Margaret Forster, Craig Raine, Giles Gordon, Mervyn Horder, John and Myfanwy Piper, Louis Lawler and David Sexton. I am particularly grateful to my friend John Wells for his translation of Verlaine's poem 'Bournemouth'. I would also like to acknowledge my debt to previous anthologists, especially Geoffrey Grigson, Hugh Kingsmill, Humphrey Jennings, Edward Phelps and Geoffrey Summerfield.

The Illustrations

More than twenty-five years ago I bought an oil painting of a Suffolk landscape in Zwemmer's Gallery off the Charing Cross Road. It was by an artist unknown to me at the time whose name was John O'Connor. I bought the painting because I liked it and because it was reasonably cheap. Some time later I met John O'Connor and we became friends almost at once. I learned to my great delight that he had been taking *Private Eye* almost from its inception. I also learned, which I did not know, that John had a high reputation as an engraver as well as a painter. Few things have given me greater pleasure than to have the opportunity to collaborate with him on this anthology. So often illustrations lead a separate existence from the text. On this occasion they spring from a common ground of friendship and shared tastes and influences.

RICHARD INGRAMS
March 1988

THE ANTHOLOGY

CLIMATE
AND SEASONS

◆§ §◆

It is commonly observed that when two Englishmen meet
their first talk is of the weather: they are in haste to tell each
other what each must already know, that it is hot or cold, bright
or cloudy, windy or calm.

SAMUEL JOHNSON, *Idler*, June 1758

There is no weather so good as English weather. Nay, in a real
sense there is no weather at all anywhere but in England. In
France you have much sun and some rain; in Italy you have hot
winds and cold winds; in Scotland and Ireland you have rain,
either thick or thin; in America you have hells of heat and cold,
and in the Tropics you have sunstrokes varied by thunderbolts.
But all these you have on a broad and brutal scale, and you
settle down into contentment or despair. Only in our own
romantic country do you have the strictly romantic thing called
Weather; beautiful and changing as a woman. The great English landscape painters (neglected now like everything that is
English) have this salient distinction: that the Weather is not
the atmosphere of their pictures; it is the subject of their pictures. They paint portraits of the Weather. The Weather sat to
Constable. The Weather posed for Turner; and a deuce of a pose
it was. This cannot truly be said of the greatest of their continental models or rivals. Poussin and Claude painted objects,
ancient cities or perfect Arcadian shepherds through a clear
medium of the climate. But in the English painters Weather is
the hero; with Turner an Adelphi hero, taunting, flashing and

fighting, melodramatic but really magnificent. The English climate, a tall and terrible protagonist, robed in rain and thunder and snow and sunlight, fills the whole canvas and the whole foreground. I admit the superiority of many other French things besides French art. But I will not yield an inch on the superiority of English weather and weather-painting. Why, the French have not even got a word for Weather; and you must ask for the weather in French as if you were asking for the time in English.

Then again, variety of climate should always go with stability of abode. The weather in the desert is monotonous; and as a natural consequence the Arabs wander about, hoping it may be different somewhere. But an Englishman's house is not only his castle; it is his fairy castle. Clouds and colours of every varied dawn and eve are perpetually touching and turning it from clay to gold, or from gold to ivory. There is a line of woodland beyond a corner of my garden which is literally different on every one of the three hundred and sixty-five days. Sometimes it seems as near as a hedge, and sometimes as far as a faint and fiery evening cloud.

G. K. CHESTERTON, 'The Glory of Grey', *Alarms and Discussions*

Winds make weather: weather
Is what nasty people are
Nasty about and the nice
Show a common joy in observing:
When I seek an image
For our Authentic City
(Across what brigs of dread,
Down what gloomy galleries,
Must we stagger or crawl
Before we may cry – O look!?)
I see old men in hallways
Tapping their barometers,
Or a lawn over which,
The first thing after breakfast,
A paterfamilias
Hurries to inspect his rain-gauge.

W. H. AUDEN, from 'Bucolics'

No two days are alike, nor even two hours; neither was there ever two leaves of a tree alike since the creation of the world.

JOHN CONSTABLE

At all times I love rain, the early momentous thunderdrops, the perpendicular cataract shining, or at night the little showers, the spongy mists, the tempestuous mountain rain. I like to see it possessing the whole earth at evening, smothering civilization, taking away from me myself everything except the power to walk under the dark trees and to enjoy as humbly as the hissing grass, while some twinkling house-light or song sung by a lonely man gives a foil to the immense dark force. I like to see the rain making the streets, the railway station, a pure desert, whether bright with lamps or not. It foams off the roofs and trees and bubbles into the water-butts. It gives the grey rivers a demonic majesty. It scours the roads, sets the flints moving, and exposes the glossy chalk in the tracks through the woods. It does work that will last as long as the earth. It is about eternal business. In its noise and myriad aspect I feel the mortal beauty of immortal things. And then after many days the rain ceases at midnight with the wind, and in the silence of dawn and frost the last rose of the world is dropping her petals down to the glistering whiteness, and there they rest blood-red on the winter's desolate coast.

EDWARD THOMAS, The South Country

13 March [1789]. Snow in the night: snow five inches deep. Snow melts on the roofs very fast: & runs thro' the ceiling of the garret.

15 March. Snow on the ground. Raw & cold. Mrs Clement left us.

16 March. Mended the cucumber frames.

17 March. Icicles hang in eaves all day. Snow melts in the sun.

19 March. Snow lies on the hill. Made the bearing cucumber-bed: the dung is full wet, but warm.

26 March. Icicles hang all day. Hot-bed smokes.

28 March. Snow did not lie. Apricots begin to blow. Earthed the nearing cucumber-bed. The plants in the seedling-bed grow, & want room. N. Aurora.

30 March. Sowed dwarf lark-spurs.

31 March. Sowed a crop of onions, lettuce, & radishes.

1 April. Rain in the night, spring-like. Crocus's make a gaudy show. Some little snow under the hedges.

3 April. Some wood-cocks are now found in Hartley-wood: as soon as the weather grows a little warm, they will pair, & leave us.

5 April. Wry-neck pipes. The smallest *uncrested wren* chirps loudly, & sharply in the hanger.

6 April. Timothy the tortoise heaves up the sod under which he is buried. Daffodil blows.

9 April. Brimstone butter-fly. The tortoise comes out. Dog violets blow. Summer like.

GILBERT WHITE, *A Naturalist's Journal*

20 March [1798]. Coleridge dined with us. We went more than half way home with him in the evening. A very cold evening, but clear. The spring seemingly very little advanced. No green trees, only the hedges are budding, and looking very lovely.

21 March. We drank tea at Coleridge's. A quiet shower of snow was in the air during more than half our walk. At our return the sky partially shaded with clouds. The horned moon was set. Startled two night birds from the great elm tree.

22 March. I spent the morning in starching and hanging out linen; walked *through* the wood in the evening, very cold.

23 March. Coleridge dined with us. He brought his ballad finished. We walked with him to the Miner's house. A beautiful evening, very starry, the horned moon.

24 March. Coleridge, the Chesters, and Ellen Cruikshank called. We walked with them through the wood. Went in the evening into the Coombe to get eggs; returned through the wood, and walked in the park. A duller night than last night: a sort of white shade over the blue sky. The stars dim. The spring continues to advance very slowly, no green trees, the hedges leafless; nothing green but the brambles that still retain their old leaves, the evergreens, and the palms, which indeed are not absolutely green. Some brambles I observed to-day budding afresh, and those have shed their old leaves. The crooked arm of the old oak tree points upwards to the moon.

25 March. Walked to Coleridge's after tea. Arrived at home at one o'clock. The night cloudy but not dark.

26 March. Went to meet Wedgwood at Coleridge's after dinner. Reached home at half-past twelve, a fine moonlight night; half moon.

27 March. Dined at Poole's. Arrived at home a little after twelve, a partially cloudy, but light night, very cold.

28 March. Hung out the linen.

29 March. Coleridge dined with us.

30 March. Walked I know not where.

31 March. Walked.

1 April. Walked by moonlight.

DOROTHY WORDSWORTH, *Journals*

It was in the middle of spring that I disembarked near London. The sky was cloudless, as in the loveliest days of Southern France; the air was cooled by a gentle west wind, which increased the clear peacefulness of nature and inclined men's minds to joy . . . I landed near Greenwich, on the banks of the Thames . . . Close to the river on a large greensward which extends for about four miles, I saw an immense number of comely young people caracoling on horseback round a kind of race-course . . . I was fortunate enough to meet in the crowd some merchants to whom I had letters of introduction. These gentlemen did me the honours of the fête with the eagerness and cordiality of men who are enjoying themselves and who are glad that others share their pleasure. They got me a horse; they sent for refreshments; they took trouble to put me in a place where I could easily see all the incidents in the races, with the river close by, and a view of London in the distance . . .

In a coffee-house which was dirty, ill-furnished, ill-served and ill-lighted, I found next day most of these gentlemen who had the day before been so affable and good-humoured. Not one of them recognized me. I ventured to enter upon conversation with some of them, but I could not get a word in reply, or at the very most, a 'Yes' or a 'No'. It seemed that on the previous day I must have done something to offend them all. I examined myself. I tried to remember if I had not expressed a preference for the manufactures of Lyons, or if I had not said that the French cooks were better than the English; that Paris was a more agreeable town than London; that the time passed more pleasantly at Versailles than at St James's, or anything else equally horrible. But I could find no guilt in myself, and so, in a lively way which seemed to them very extraordinary, I ventured to ask them, why they were all so miserable. One of them sulkily replied that the wind was in the east.

At this moment one of their friends came in and said quite indifferently: 'Molly cut her throat this morning; her lover found her dead in her room with a blood-stained razor beside her.' This Molly was a young, beautiful, and very rich girl, about to be married to the very man who had found her dead. These gentlemen who were all her friends, received the news

22

without wincing. One of them merely asked what had become of the lover. He has bought the razor, was the cold reply.

I was aghast at so strange a death and appalled by these Englishmen's indifference. I could not refrain from asking what could have driven a young lady, seemingly so happy, to tear herself cruelly from life. I got no other answer than that the wind was in the east. I could not at first understand what the east wind had to do with the melancholy mood of these gentlemen and with the death of Molly. I abruptly left the coffee-house and went to the Court, pleasantly presuming, in my natural French way, that a Court was always gay. But gloom and wretchedness possessed everything there, even the very maids of honour themselves. They said in a melancholy way that the wind was in the east. Then I thought of the Dane I had met the day before. I felt a temptation to laugh at the false idea which he had carried away with him from England; but the influence of the climate had already begun to work upon me, and I was astonished to find that I could not laugh. A famous court doctor to whom I mentioned my surprise, told me that I ought not to be astonished yet; that I would see a very different state of things in November and in March, when the people hung themselves by the dozen; that almost everyone was ill during those two seasons, and that a cloud of melancholy hung over the nation. 'For,' said he, 'those are the months when the east wind blows most obstinately. That wind is the ruin of our island. The very animals suffer from it and have a woebegone look. The men who are strong enough to keep their health in this cursed wind at least lose their good-humour. Everyone looks stern and cross and is disposed to form desperate resolutions. It was precisely in an east wind that Charles I was beheaded and that James II was dethroned. If you have any favour to ask at Court,' he added in my ear, 'never go ask it unless the wind is in the west or south.'

Voltaire's England

April Days

The first of April 1769 was the Coldest Day that had been felt since the first of January – odd enough!

The first of May the same year 1769 was as remarkably hot,

the Trees in full verdure, the Dust flying and one's friends kicking out their carpets, & running into the country.

On the sixteenth of April 1771 it froze exceedingly hard, there was ice in all the Channels and no appearance of Spring even in the neighbourhood of London.

On the 2d of April 1774 the Trees are busting out – not into bloom but into leaf, one cannot bear a fire in the Room and London is as disagreeable from Heat and Dust as in July –

The 2d April 1775 was a day remarkably warm & fine: the trees are all in Bloom, some in Leafe, & summer seems already far advanced.

On the 13th April 1775 we had a violent *Summer Storm* of Thunder Lightning and Rain, the Heat & Storm & everything reminded one of July.

21st April 1775 I returned home from Southwark to Streatham to lye in: I think it sometimes remarkable that I should fix this day six months ago & be able to keep it so exactly. The cuckoo sung all the way home.

MRS THRALE, *Thraliana*

Kelmscott
Easter Monday

The country is about six weeks backward; more backward by a good deal than it was last year, though that was late: neither the big trees (except the chestnuts) nor the apple trees show any sign of life yet. The garden is very pretty, though there are scarcely any flowers in blossom except the primroses; but there are such beautiful promises of buds and things just out of the ground that it makes amends for all. The buds of the wild tulip, which is one of the beautifullest flowers there is, just at point to open. Jenny and I went up to Buscot wood this morning: it is such a change from our river plain that it is like going into another country; yet I don't much care about a wood unless it is a very big one; and Buscot is scarcely more than a coppice; but the blue distance between the trunks was very beautiful. As to the weather, bearing in mind that things are so much behindhand, it is not bad. Today has been March all over; rain-showers, hail, wind, dead calm, thunder, finishing with a calm

frosty evening sky. The birds are amusing, especially the starlings, whereof there are many: but some damned fool has been
bullying our rooks so much that they have only got six nests, so
that we haven't got the proper volume of sound from them.

One grief, the sort of thing that is always happening in the
spring: there were some beautiful willows at Eaton Hastings
which to my certain knowledge had not been polled during the
whole 17 years that we have been here; and now the idiot Parson has polled them into wretched stumps. I should like to cut
off the beggar's legs and have wooden ones made for him out of
the willow timber, the value of which is about 7s. 6d.

WILLIAM MORRIS, letter to Mrs Burne-Jones, 1889

May 1861. Today, Thursday, is like yesterday – thorough influ-
enza weather. East wind, damp, cold, and fog, and the top of a
tree in Kensington Gardens is but just visible. The gloom just
now is overpowering, the London smoke is hovering over like
a pall. The cold weather makes one's fingers ache after washing . . .

Half-past eight. The darkness increases, and the foul smells
of London come in through every crevice . . .

SAMUEL PALMER

Spring

Nothing is so beautiful as spring –
   When weeds, in wheels, shoot long and lovely and lush;
   Thrush's eggs look little low heavens, and thrush
Through the echoing timber does so rinse and wring
The ear, it strikes like lightnings to hear him sing;
   The glassy peartree leaves and blooms, they brush
   The descending blue; that blue is all in a rush
With richness; the racing lambs too have fair their fling.

What is all this juice and all this joy?
    A strain of the earth's sweet being in the beginning
In Eden Garden. – Have, get, before it cloy,
    Before it cloud, Christ, lord, and sour with sinning,
Innocent mind and Mayday in girl and boy,
    Most, O maid's child, thy choice and worthy the winning.

GERARD MANLEY HOPKINS

Sunday 7 May [1871]. I went to church early, soon after ten o'clock, across the quiet sunny meadows. There was scarcely anyone about – only one boy loitering by the stile in Becks by the road under the elms. The trees are in their most exquisite and perfect loveliness. There is usually one day in the Spring when the beauty of everything culminates and strikes one peculiarly, even forcing itself upon one's notice and a presentiment comes that one will never see such loveliness again at least for another year. This is the day that Robert Burns delighted in, the first fine Sunday in May. He had a peculiar love for such a day as this. The great elms shaded the road from the glowing sunshine and everything was still and beautiful and green.

I went into the churchyard under the feathering larch which sweeps over the gate. The ivy-grown old church with its noble tower stood beautiful and silent among the elms with its graves at its feet. Everything was still. No one was about or moving and the only sound was the singing of birds. The place was all in a charm of singing, full of peace and quiet sunshine. It seemed to be given up to the birds and their morning hymns. It was the bird church, the church among the birds. I wandered round the church among the dewy grass-grown graves and picturesque ivy- and moss-hung tombstones. Round one grave grew a bed of primroses. Upon another tall cowslips hung their heads.

The hour for service drew on. The clerk coughed in the church. Two girls in grey dresses passed quietly through the church and moved about among the graves on the N. side bending over a grave beneath the elm. Then a woman in deep mourning moved slowly down the path of the churchyard, and the clerk began to ring the bell for service. My Father read prayers and I preached on the Master washing the disciples' feet.

FRANCIS KILVERT, *Diaries*

Cut Grass

Cut grass lies frail:
Brief is the breath
Mown stalks exhale.
Long, long the death

It dies in the white hours
Of young-leafed June
With chestnut flowers,
With hedges snowlike strewn,

White lilac bowed,
Lost lanes of Queen Anne's lace,
And that high-builded cloud
Moving at summer's pace.

PHILIP LARKIN

It was hot; and after walking some time over the gardens in a scattered, dispersed way, scarcely any three together, they insensibly followed one another to the delicious shade of a broad short avenue of limes, which stretching beyond the garden at an equal distance from the river, seemed the finish of the pleasure grounds. – It led to nothing; nothing but a view at the end of a low stone wall with high pillars, which seemed intended, in their erection, to give the appearance of an approach to the house, which never had been there. Disputable, however, as might be the taste of such a termination, it was in itself a charming walk, and the view which closed it extremely pretty. – The considerable slope, at nearly the foot of which the Abbey stood, gradually acquired a steeper form beyond its grounds; and at half a mile distant was a bank of considerable abruptness and grandeur, well clothed with wood; – and at the bottom of this bank, favourably placed and sheltered, rose the Abbey-Mill Farm, with meadows in front, and the river making a close and handsome curve around it.

It was a sweet view – sweet to the eye and the mind. English verdure, English culture, English comfort, seen under a sun bright, without being oppressive.

JANE AUSTEN, *Emma*

Summer *cold* in June. Shivering in the evenings in the parlour with lilac and flowers in the grate and apple bloom in the garden. Yet cold, and all the green things dripping.

RICHARD JEFFERIES, *Nature Diaries*, 1878

Summer

So, some tempestuous morn in early June,
    When the year's primal burst of bloom is o'er,
        Before the roses and the longest day –
    When garden-walks, and all the grassy floor,
        With blossoms, red and white, of fallen May,
            And chestnut-flowers are strewn –
So have I heard the cuckoo's parting cry,
        From the wet field, through the vext garden-trees,
        Come with the volleying rain and tossing breeze:
The bloom is gone, and with the bloom go I.

Too quick despairer, wherefore wilt thou go?
  Soon will the high Midsummer pomps come on,
    Soon will the musk carnations break and swell,
  Soon shall we have gold-dusted snapdragon,
    Sweet-William with its homely cottage smell,
      And stocks in fragrant blow;
  Roses that down the alleys shine afar,
    And open, jasmine-muffled lattices,
    And groups under the dreaming garden-trees,
  And the full moon, and the white evening-star.

MATTHEW ARNOLD, from 'Thyrsis'

9 June 1802 [Grasmere] . . . The hawthorns on the mountain-sides like orchards in blossom . . .

13 June. A fine morning. Sunshiny and bright, but with rainy clouds . . .

15 June. A sweet grey, mild morning. The birds sing soft and low . . .

16 June . . . I do not now see the brownness that was in the coppices. The lower hawthorn blossoms passed away. Those on the hills are a faint white. The wild guelder rose is coming out, and the wild roses. I have seen no honey-suckles yet . . . Foxgloves are now frequent.

20 June . . . We were in the orchard a great part of the morning. After tea we walked upon our own path for a long time. We talked sweetly together about the disposal of our riches. We lay upon the sloping turf. Earth and sky were so lovely that they melted our very hearts. The sky to the north was of a chastened yet rich yellow, fading into pale blue, and streaked and scattered over with steady islands of purple, melting away into shades of pink. It was like a vision to me . . .

DOROTHY WORDSWORTH, *Journals*

Out of the thirty days of June, fourteen were wet at my station near London. There was heavy rain very early in the morning of another day, and distant thunder on another; nor does this include several days when there was only a sprinkling of rain. Moreover, there was much rain during the nights; and such days as were dry were often overcast and gloomy. The longest day came in with steady rain; the afternoon, though dry, was cloudy, and the evening closed with a wind that howled down the chimneys like a true winter blast. Midsummer Day was wild and rough, and will best be described by the entries made at the time: 'Rain in early morning; fine afterwards till noon, then heavy showers with intervals of blue sky; afterwards thunder, heavy rain, hail, and rough gusts of wind sending the leaves spinning away.' Next day there was more heavy rain, with thunder and flashes of lightning visible about noon. But the wildest day of all was perhaps the 1st of July: a furious gale driving a heavy rain before it swept across the fields, tearing the green leaves and twigs from the trees, and scattering small branches and dead boughs. It lasted from early morning till towards afternoon, when it gradually sank, and a comparatively fine evening led people to hope that the worst was over. It is remarkable that this happened time after time – a sunset that seemed to all who had not made a study of the sky clear and promising, followed by clouded mornings. And when a fine day did come, the roads and pathways were still muddy, and had the appearance of recent storms. Before these could disappear, down came the rain again. There were only about five days in June that could be called really fine; and when two of these happened in succession it was regarded as quite remarkable . . . Yet the flowers have been beautiful. Those who ventured out despite the rain found the hedges in June white with the May-bloom – late but lovely. Surely the buttercups were never so numerous. The meadows were one wide expanse of gold, almost dazzling when the sun did shine.

RICHARD JEFFERIES, *Chronicles of the Hedges*

It is the first of July, and I sit down to write by the dismallest light that ever yet I wrote by, namely, the light of this mid-summer morning, in mid-England (Matlock, Derbyshire) in the year 1871.

For the sky is covered with grey cloud: not raincloud, but a dry black veil, which no ray of sunshine can pierce; partly diffused in mist, feeble mist, enough to make distant objects unintelligible, yet without any substance, or wreathing, or colour of its own. And everywhere the leaves of the trees are shaking fitfully, as they do before a thunderstorm; only not violently, but enough to show the passing to and fro of a strange, bitter, blighting wind. Dismal enough, had it been the first morning of its kind that summer had sent. But during all this spring, in London, and at Oxford, through meagre March, through changelessly sullen April, through despondent May, and darkened June, morning after morning has come grey-shrouded thus.

JOHN RUSKIN, *Fors Clavigera*

Hampstead

12 August 1920. More beautiful by far than a morning in spring or summer. The mist – the trees standing in it – not a leaf moves – not a breath stirs. There is a faint smell of burning. The sun comes slowly – slowly the room grows lighter. Suddenly, on the carpet, there is a square of pale, red light. The bird in the garden goes 'snip – snip – snip' – a little wheezy, like the sound of a knife-grinder. The nasturtiums blaze in the garden: their leaves are pale. On the lawn, his paws tucked under him, sits the black and white cat . . .

KATHERINE MANSFIELD, *Journal*

In the month of August, every year, I find that England becomes uninhabitable. Streams of people from the Midlands and the North of England come down to the West Country, usually in caravans to avoid having to spend money. Bumper to bumper, they block every road and every country lane. When they leave their caravans, clad only in shorts to relieve themselves in specially built Rest Areas, they act as a terrible reminder that the New Britain does really exist, it is not just a hideous invention of *The Sunday Times* under Harold Evans. Its problems are not my problems, its enthusiasms are not my enthusiasms. So far as I am concerned, they are total aliens, and no doubt they would find me equally alien to their own experience if they ever paused to talk to the natives in the countryside they invade, with their crates of tinned food, their cash-and-carry supplies of northern lavatory paper.

But when September comes, and we return from France, they have all disappeared. The countryside reasserts itself. Leaves begin to fall from the trees. The pheasant shooting begins. The trees are still there, so are the churches, the large houses, the familiar faces. How can one seriously worry about the future when everything around has been going on for so long? Such change as has occurred, outside the towns, has been for the most part benign: farmworkers now have hot water and electricity, even central heating in their cottages. They have television and cars. The birds and beasts – badgers, foxes, hedgehogs, rabbits, voles – go about their business, even if they are likely to be under the damp eyes of some retired animal sentimentalist from Solihull. The truth is that all the brutality and filth of modern Britain is concentrated in a few areas, at any rate for most of the year. So long as people who wish to do so can escape, there will always be an England.

AUBERON WAUGH, *Antique*

7 September 1791. Cut 125 cucumbers. Young martins, several hundreds, congregate on the tower, church and yew-tree. Hence I conclude that most of the second broods are flown. Such an assemblage is very beautiful, & amusing, did it not bring with it an association of ideas tending to make us reflect that winter is approaching; & that these little birds are consulting how they may avoid it.

9 September. Gathered in the white apples, a very fine crop of large fine fruit, consisting of many bushels.

10 September. Young broods of swallows come out. Cut 171 cucumbers; in all 424 this week. Sweet moonlight!

14 September. Hop-picking goes on without the least interruption. Stone-curlews cry late in the evenings. The congregating flocks of *hirundines* on the church & tower are very beautiful, & amusing! When they fly-off altogether from the Roof, on any alarm, they quite swarm in the air. But they soon settle in heaps, & preening their feathers, & lifting up their wings to admit the sun, seem highly to enjoy the warm situation. Thus they spend the heat of the day, preparing for their emigration, &, as it were, consulting when & where they are to go. The flight about the church seems to consist chiefly of house-martins, about 400 in number: but there are other places of rendezvous about the village frequented at the same time. The swallows seem to delight more in holding their assemblies on trees.

GILBERT WHITE, *A Naturalist's Journal*

We too have been having a Fortnight of delightful weather, so as one has been able to sit abroad all the Day. And now, that Spirit which Tennyson sung of in one of his early Poems is heard, as it were, walking and talking to himself among the decaying flower-beds. This Season (such as we have been enjoying) – my old Crabbe sings of it too, in a very pathetic way to me: for it always seems to me an Image of the Decline of Life also.

> It was a Day ere yet the Autumn closed,
> When Earth before her Winter's War reposed;

When from the Garden as we look'd above,
No Cloud was seen, and nothing seem'd to move . . .
When the wing'd Insect settled in our sight,
And waited wind to recommence its flight.

EDWARD FITZGERALD, *Letters*, 15 October 1878

The Burning of the Leaves

Now is the time for the burning of the leaves.
They go to the fire; the nostril pricks with smoke
Wandering slowly into a weeping mist.
Brittle and blotched, ragged and rotten sheaves!
A flame seizes the smouldering ruin and bites
On stubborn stalks that crackle as they resist.

The last hollyhock's fallen tower is dust;
All the spices of June are a bitter reek,
All the extravagant riches spent and mean.
All burns! The reddest rose is a ghost;
Sparks whirl up, to expire in the mist: the wild
Fingers of fire are making corruption clean.

Now is the time for stripping the spirit bare,
Time for the burning of days ended and done,
Idle solace of things that have gone before:
Rootless hope and fruitless desire are there;
Let them go to the fire, with never a look behind.
The world that was ours is a world that is ours no more.

They will come again, the leaf and the flower, to arise
From squalor of rottenness into the old splendour,
And magical scents to a wondering memory bring;
The same glory, to shine upon different eyes.
Earth cares for her own ruins, naught for ours.
Nothing is certain, only the certain spring.

LAURENCE BINYON

Song

Fall, leaves, fall; die, flowers, away;
Lengthen night and shorten day;
Every leaf speaks bliss to me
Fluttering from the autumn tree.
I shall smile when wreaths of snow
Blossom where the rose should grow;
I shall sing when night's decay
Ushers in a drearier day.

EMILY BRONTË

Winter at Home

Now comes the time when gardeners have given up trying to sweep away leaves. We have taken the honesty out of the top shelf in the linen cupboard and stuck it in the brass altar vases of the village church. Last Sunday the last of the Michaelmas daisies were too frost-bitten to be conducive to public worship. Now England, having got rid of tourists and those who feel they must seek sunlight, settles down to be herself. With any luck there will be fogs in November and December so that the sky will not be poisoned with aeroplanes and a quiet of eternity will be about us, just the drip drip from wet branches and smells of wood-smoke and fungus in the lanes . . .

Ah, the sweet prelude to an English winter! For me it is so much a more beautiful season than any other, which is just as well since it goes on for most of the year. It is a time when there is more colour in the country than there was ever before. Ploughed fields take on a look like a farming scene in the initial letter of a medieval manuscript. Bricks are an intenser red and Cotswold stone is more golden, the limestone and granite of the north is more silver, bare branches are like pressed seaweed against the pale blue sky. Whatever remains green is more deeply, richly green than it was before. This waiting, intense stillness is generally a prelude to a storm. The smallest sound is easily heard. Cocks are continually crowing, ducks quacking as though they were happy, and even across three miles of still, misty fields, it is possible to distinguish all six of the church bells as men practise method ringing in the oil-lit evening tower. But this night there is not one of those gigantic winter sunsets and the house is more than usually full of spiders, huge hairy ones which cast a shadow twice their own size on the drawing-room carpet. And then, in the night the storm begins. Will the trees stand it, this gale which makes them roar and creak and roar again? Will the earth ever be able to soak up these torrents which beat the house, brim the water-butts and swish on grass and gravel? And has anyone remembered to shut the upstairs window?

JOHN BETJEMAN, *First and Last Loves*

I see the winter approaching without much concern, though a passionate lover of fine weather and the pleasant scenes of summer; but the long evenings have their comforts too, and there is hardly to be found upon the earth, I suppose, so snug a creature as an Englishman by his fireside in the winter. I mean however an Englishman that lives in the country, for in London it is not very easy to avoid intrusion.

WILLIAM COWPER, letter to Joseph Hill, 20 October 1783

It is now the 8th of December: it has blown a most desperate East wind, all razors; a wind like one of those knives one sees in a shop in London, with 365 blades all drawn and pointed . . .

EDWARD FITZGERALD, *Letters*, 1844

O, thought I! What a beautiful thing God has made winter to be, by stripping the trees, and letting us see their shapes and forms.

DOROTHY WORDSWORTH, *Journals*, 1802

23 December 1890. Was awakened this morning at 9.30 by man outside bellowing 'Execution of Mrs Pearcy! Scene on the Scaffold! – Paper!' (I suppose the execution was at 8 o'clock, so that the paper must have been got out speedily). Such cries harmonized with the morning; snow lying everywhere grimy with soot, & a muddy fog obscuring the sky. Yesterday one of the most hideous fogs I ever knew, unintermittent. One might describe the weather, & connect it with reflections on capital punishment.

GEORGE GISSING, *Commonplace Book*

Winter brings natural inducements to jollity and conversation. Differences, we know, are never so effectively laid asleep, as by some common calamity; an enemy unites all to whom he threatens danger. The rigour of winter brings generally to the same fireside those who, by the opposition of inclinations, in difference of employment moved in various directions through the other parts of the year; and when they have met, and find it their mutual interest to remain together, they endear each other by mutual compliances, and often wish for the continuance of the social season, with all its blackness and all its severities.

To men of study and imagination the winter is generally the chief time of labour. Gloom and silence produce composure of mind, and concentration of ideas: and the privation of external pleasure naturally causes an effect to find entertainment within. This is the time in which those whom literature enables to find amusements for themselves, have more than common convictions of their own happiness. When they are condemned by the elements to retirement, and debarred from most of the diversions which are called in to assist the flight of time, they can find new subjects of enquiry, and preserve themselves from that weariness which hangs always flagging upon the vacant mind.

SAMUEL JOHNSON, *Rambler*, December 1750

PLACES

◗§ §◖

The charm of England is the vast variety of scenery,
atmosphere, everything in small spaces. Think of the variety of
country close on each of the great towns. Compare the
surroundings of London with those of Paris or Berlin. And
everywhere the sea is near.

GEORGE GISSING, *Commonplace Book*

Wessex guidebook

Hayfoot; strawfoot; the illiterate seasons
Still clump their way through Somerset and Dorset
While George the Third still rides his horse of chalk
From Weymouth and the new salt water cure
Towards Windsor and incurable madness. Inland
The ghosts of monks have grown too fat to walk
Through bone-dry ruins plugged with fossil sea-shells.

Thou shalt! Thou shalt not! In the yellow abbey
Inscribed beneath the crossing the Ten Commandments
Are tinted red by a Fifteenth-Century fire;
On one round hill the yews still furnish bows
For Agincourt while, equally persistent,
Beneath another, in green-grassed repose,
Arthur still waits the call to rescue Britain.

Flake-tool; core-tool; in the small museum
Rare butterflies, green coins of Caracalla,
Keep easy company with the fading hand
Of one who chronicled a fading world;
Outside, the long roads, that the Roman ruler
Ruled himself out with, point across the land
To lasting barrows and long-vanished barracks.

And thatchpoll numskull rows of limestone houses,
Dead from the navel down in plate-glass windows,
Despise their homebrewed past, ignore the clock
On the village church in deference to Big Ben
Who booms round china dog and oaken settle
Announcing it is time and time again
To plough up tumuli, to damn the hindmost.

But hindmost, topmost, those illiterate seasons
Still smoke their pipes in swallow-hole and hide-out
As scornful of the tractor and the jet
As of the Roman road, or axe of flint,
Forgotten by the mass of human beings
Whom they, the Seasons, need not even forget
Since, though they fostered man, they never loved him.

LOUIS MACNEICE

Great Houses

A number of these great houses are historical: only by seeing
them can one realize what inheritance from generation to
generation can accumulate in the way of treasures, in a great
family. I have been told of one in which, by a clause in the
entail, the owner is obliged to spend several thousand pounds a
year on silverware. After having crammed all the sideboards,
they resorted to having the banister of the staircase made of

solid silver. In the late Exhibition I saw a whole museum of valuable curios and *objets d'art* loaned by Lord Hertford. In 1848 the same nobleman, talking to a Frenchman who was a friend of his and was in serious difficulties, said,

'I have a place in Wales which I have never seen but they tell me it's very fine. A dinner for twelve is served there every day, and the carriage brought round to the door, in case I should arrive. It's the butler who eats the dinner. Go and settle down there; as you see, it will not cost me a farthing.'

Naturally, beautiful things tend to accumulate in wealthy hands. Miss Coots (*sic*), Lord Ellesmere, and the Marquis of Westminster own picture galleries which would do honour to a small nation. At Lord Ellesmere's, in three rooms as lofty as the Louvre gallery, are a quantity of Poussins, the best Flemish painters, and, above all, three medium-sized Titians, *Diana and Acteon*, *Diana and Calypso*, and *Venus rising from the waves*, of a warm golden colour and a most opulent and vivid beauty. At the Marquis of Westminster's, two galleries and four enormous rooms, one hundred and eighty-three pictures and a whole *cortège* of busts, statues, bronzes, enamel and malachite pieces; six large Rubens, three Titians, a Raphael, two Rembrandts and a quantity of Claude Lorrains chosen from among his best works. And these palaces are only quoted as specimens, it would take too long to give an idea of the whole number.

In the course of another trip I saw Blenheim Castle, near Woodstock, property of the Duke of Marlborough. It is a sort of Louvre, and was given by the nation to the great general, the first duke. It is built in the style of that time, heavily ornamented. Several of the rooms are as lofty as the nave of a church; the library is a hundred yards long; an interior chapel contains the first duke's monument. There is a gallery of family portraits, another of porcelain, and several galleries of pictures. The park is two miles in circumference. Magnificent trees, a wide watercourse crossed by a monumental bridge, a column bearing the first duke's statue. There is a private room containing, under the name of Titian, twelve copies, the Loves of the Gods, voluptuous, life-sized figures: they were presented to the victor of Louis XIV by the princes of Italy. The apartments contain paintings by Reynolds, five or six large Van Dyck portraits, a Raphael Madonna and ten Rubens in which sensuality, passion, boldness and genius pour out a whole river of splendours and enormities. Two of these are Bacchanals: a colossal female faun has thrown herself down on the ground and sits stooped above her dropping dugs, and her two young, lying on their backs and glued to her nipples, are sucking avidly, the whole a great jumble of palpitating flesh; above, the dark torso of Silenus throws into relief the dazzling whiteness of a strapping, hoydenish, writhing nymph; nearby is another Silenus, bronzed and enormous, laughing a drunkard's laugh, dancing with all his heart and might so that his paunch is bouncing about, while a beautiful young woman, resting on her hip, displays the long, undulating lines of side and breasts. I would not dare to describe the third picture, the most vivid of all, of a sublime grossness, the very sap and flower of irrepressible passionate sensuality, the whole poetry of drunkenness unrestrained and bestial satiety; the title, *Lot and his two daughters.* But I am forgetting myself; these memories, like a gust of warm air, have made me digress. The conclusion I have been aiming at is that these great hereditary fortunes are as if designed to preserve these and all treasures of beauty. After a number of generations a great house and park become a casket of gems.

HIPPOLYTE TAINE, *Notes on England*

Salisbury Cathedral

Swallows, martins, and swifts were numerous, the martins especially, and it was beautiful to see them for ever wheeling about in a loose swarm about the building. They reminded me of bees and flies, and sometimes with a strong light on them they were like those small polished black and silvery-white beetles (*Gyrinus*) which we see in companies on the surface of pools and streams, perpetually gliding and whirling about in a sort of complicated dance. They looked very small at a height of a couple of hundred feet from the ground, and their smallness and numbers and lively and eccentric motions made them very insect-like.

The starlings and sparrows were in a small minority among the breeders, but including these there were seven species in all, and as far as I could make out numbered about three hundred and fifty birds – probably the largest wild-bird colony on any building in England.

Nor could birds in all this land find a more beautiful building to nest on, unless I except Wells Cathedral solely on account of its west front, beloved of daws, and where their numerous black company have so fine an appearance. Wells has its west front; Salisbury, so vast in size, is yet a marvel of beauty in its entirety; and seeing it as I now did every day and wanting nothing better, I wondered at my want of enthusiasm on a previous visit. Still, to me, the bird company, the sight of their airy gambols and their various voices, from the deep human-like dove tones to the perpetual subdued rippling, running-water sound of the aerial martins, must always be a principal element in the beautiful effect. Nor do I know a building where Nature has done more in enhancing the loveliness of man's work with her added colouring. The way too in which the colours are distributed is an example of Nature's most perfect artistry; on the lower, heavier buttressed parts, where the darkest hues should be, we find the browns and rust-reds of the minute aerial alga, mixed with the greys of lichen, these darker stainings extending upwards to a height of fifty or sixty feet, in places higher, then giving place to more delicate hues, the pale tender greens and greenish greys, in places tinged with yellow, the colours always appearing brightest on the smooth surface between the windows and sculptured parts. The effect depends a good deal on atmosphere and weather: on a day of flying clouds and a blue sky, with a brilliant sunshine on the vast building after a shower, the colouring is most beautiful. It varies more than in the case of colour in the material itself or of pigments, because it is a 'living' colour, as Crabbe rightly says in his lumbering verse:

> The living stains, which Nature's hand alone,
> Profuse of life, pours out upon the stone.

Greys, greens, yellows, and browns and rust-reds are but the colours of a variety of lowly vegetable forms, mostly lichens and the aerial alga called iolithus.

Without this colouring, its 'living stains', Salisbury would not have fascinated me as it did during this last visit. It would have left me cold though all the architects and artists had assured me that it was the most perfectly beautiful building on earth.

I also found an increasing charm in the interior, and made the discovery that I could go oftener and spend more hours in this cathedral without a sense of fatigue or depression than in any other one known to me, because it has less of that peculiar character which we look for and almost invariably find in our cathedrals. It has not the rich sombre majesty, the dim religious light and heavy vault-like atmosphere of the other great fanes. So airy and light is it that it is almost like being out of doors. You do not experience that instantaneous change, as of a curtain being drawn excluding the light and air of day and of being shut in, which you have on entering other religious houses. This is due, first, to the vast size of the interior, the immense length of the nave, and the unobstructed view one has inside owing to the removal by the 'vandal' Wyatt of the old ponderous stone screen – an act for which I bless while all others curse his memory; secondly, to the comparatively small amount of stained glass there is to intercept the light. So graceful and beautiful is the interior that it can bear the light, and light suits it best, just as a twilight best suits Exeter and Winchester and other cathedrals with heavy sculptured roofs. One marvels at a building so vast in size which yet produces the effect of a palace in fairyland, or of a cathedral not built with hands but brought into existence by a miracle.

I began to think it not safe to stay in that place too long, lest it should compel me to stay there always or cause me to feel dissatisfied and homesick when away.

W. H. HUDSON, *Afoot in England*

Totnes

It was nightfall when I quitted the train at Totnes station, and walked off alone along a dark bit of road under the stars, to enter a strange town – a special delight; turned a corner, into the long, narrow, roughly paved High Street; downhill, to the poetic sign The Seven Stars, a large, old-fashioned hostel, with garden to the river; then, after choosing bedroom, out again for the never-to-be-omitted-when-possible immediate and rapid survey, by any sort of light, of the place not seen before since I was born.

Up-hill goes the steep, narrow street, crossed, half way up, by a deep arch bearing a house; then the houses on each side jut on the side path supported on stumpy stone pillars; then I zig-zag to the left, still upwards, and by and by come to the last house, and the last lamp, throwing its gleam on the hedgerows and trees of a solitary country road. This last house was an old and sizable one, with mullioned windows, one of which is lighted, and on the blind falls a shadow from within of a woman sewing. The slight and placid movements of this figure, at once so shadowy and so real, so close at hand and so remote, are suggestive of rural contentment, a life of security and quietude. Yet how different from this the facts may be!

WILLIAM ALLINGHAM, *Diary*

The Vale of Severn

The sudden variation from the hill country of Gloucestershire to the Vale of Severn, as observed from Birdlip, or Frowcester Hill, is strikingly sublime. You travel for twenty or five-and-twenty miles over one of the most unfortunate, desolate countries under heaven, divided by stone walls, and abandoned to screaming kites and larcenous crows: after travelling really twenty, and to appearance ninety miles over this region of stone and sorrow, life begins to be a burden, and you wish to perish. At the very moment when you are taking this melancholy view of human affairs, and hating the postilion, and blaming the horses, there bursts upon your view, with all its towers, forests, and streams, the deep and shaded Vale of Severn. Sterility and nakedness are thrown in the background: as far as the eye can reach, all is comfort, opulence, product, and beauty: now it is an ancient city, or a fair castle rising out of the forests, and now the beautiful Severn is noticed winding among the cultivated fields, and the cheerful habitations of men. The train of mournful impressions is quite effaced, and you descend rapidly into a vale of plenty, with a heart full of wonder and delight.

SYDNEY SMITH

I really enjoyed my journey to and fro Yarmouth. I got there on the most beautiful evening with the low sun setting over the great flats. The country is most curious about there: the great alluvial flats with their rivers and wide ditches are bounded by low banks of sand and gravel grown over by heather and ling and bracken as if you were in a mountainous country: and then there is the fen almost on a level with you. The town itself is very pleasant: the little 'rows' in which all the workmen and most of the others live, open out into a huge market place: above the town the river widens into a kind of lake (called Bredon) which is, of course, tidal: the harbour is made by the river defended from the sea by a long low bank of sand. It was full of ships and smacks; we walked two miles along it yesterday, and watched the smacks being tugged out to sea, for the herring fishery is now beginning. I am sorry to say that the fishermen are terribly exploited by the capitalists and all very badly off . . .

WILLIAM MORRIS, letter to Jane Morris, 30 August 1889

Berkhamsted

I returned to the little town a while ago – it was Sunday evening and the bells were jangling; small groups of youths hovered round the traffic lights, while the Irish servant girls crept out of back doors in the early dark. They were 'Romans', but they were impertinent to the priest if he met them in the high street away from the small, too new Catholic church in one of the red-brick villaed streets above the valley. They couldn't be kept in at night. They would return with the milk in a stranger's car. The youths with smarmed and scented hair and bitten cigarettes greeted them by the traffic lights with careless roughness. There were so many fish in the sea . . . sexual experience had come to them too early and too easily. . . .

I walked down towards my old home, down the dim drab high street, between the estate agents', the two cinemas, the cafés; there existed still faint signs of the old market town –

there was a crusader's helmet in the church. People are made by places, I thought; I called this 'home', and sentiment moved in the winter evening, but it had no real hold. Smoke waved in the sky behind the Tudor Café and showed the 8.52 was in. You couldn't live in a place like this – it was somewhere to which you returned for sleep and rissoles by the 6.50 or the 7.25; people had lived here once and died with their feet crossed to show they had returned from a crusade, but now . . . Yellowing faces peered out of the photographer's window, through the diamonded Elizabethan pane – a genuine pane, but you couldn't believe it because of the Tudor Café across the street. I saw a face I knew in a wedding group, but it had been taken ten years before – there was something *démodé* about the waistcoat. With a train every hour to town there wasn't much reason to be photographed here – except, of course, for passports in a hurry. . . .

In the morning, mist lay heavy on the Chilterns. Boards marking desirable building lots dripped on short grass, and the skeletons of harrows lay unburied on the wet stubble. With visibility shut down to fifty yards you got no sense of a world, of simultaneous existences: each thing was self-contained like an image of private significance, standing for something else – Metroland loneliness. The door of the Plough Inn chimed when you pushed it, ivory balls clicked, and a bystander said, 'They do this at the Crown, Margate' – England's heart beating out in bagatelle towards her eastern extremity. In a small front garden before a red villa a young girl knelt in the damp with an expression abased and secretive while she sawed through the limbs of a bush, the saw wailing through wet wood, and a woman's angry voice called, 'Judy, Judy,' and a dog barked in the poultry farm across the way. A cigarette fumed into ash with no one in sight near a little shut red door marked 'Ker Even'.

The cairn terrier farm stood on the crest of the hill. The dogs can never have been quiet; masculine women holding big steel combs strode in tweeds past the kennels. A notice said, 'Mazawattee Tea'. Bungalows were to let. Among the beech woods a brand new house was advertised for sale. It had been built with dignity as if to last, as though it stood for something – if only the pride of ownership. But it had been lived in only a month; the woods and commons were held out precariously by wire. The owner had married in December and had been divorced in August; they had seen one of each season – except for autumn – and neither wanted the house to live in afterwards. A handyman swept up the beech leaves from the paths – a losing fight against the woods – and lamented the waste of it all.

'Four coats of paint in every room . . . I was going to make a pool in the dell down there – another month and I'd have got the kitchen garden straight.'

GRAHAM GREENE, The Lawless Roads

The Cotswolds

Blockley nestles, as Broad Campden does, and Shipston on Stour. The wolds encase them: lazy undulations, fields guarded by trim stone walls. Patches of sheep whiten the hilly sward, poppies blaze through a field of rye. In the July sunshine the roadside verges are a yard high, yellowing cow-parsley sprinkled with crane's-bill and campion. Elder fills the hedgerows.

In Stow on the Wold you pass down an ancient passage to the Gents, and the hard black oak of door-frames seems tougher than the ubiquitous stone. Above hotels and pubs the wrought-iron signs are motionless on a tranquil afternoon. 'The real McCoy!' an American cyclist proclaims, pausing in one town or another, it doesn't matter which. Tea-rooms are full of shortbread and Bendicks' chocolate mint crisps, part of the scenery.

Domestic pastoral: the Cotswold scene is that, the stone of houses is the stone of the wolds, and Cotswold faces are part of nature too. At dusk, old women in summer dresses make the journey through their village to look at someone else's flowers. At dawn, unshaven itinerants move dourly through the fields from one farm to the next. With passing years, these small conventions remain, even if Northwick Park has become a business school and Blockley's silk mills are bijou residences now. The Gloucestershire voice hasn't altered much, either: on market day in Moreton in Marsh it's matter-of-fact and firm, without the lilt that sweetens it further west. Like the countryside it speaks for, its tones are undramatic, as if constantly aware that life owes much to sheep, that least theatrical of animals. While landscape and buildings merge, nobody who lives here is likely to forget that the riches and good sense of wool merchants created the Cotswolds.

When I walk in England I walk in Dartmoor or Derbyshire, and I have chosen Devon to live in. I like the English seaside out of season, Budleigh Salterton and Bexhill; it is Somerset I watch playing cricket. But best of all in England there's Gloucestershire to visit and to stroll through, while pheasants rise elegantly from its parklands and rivers modestly make their way. No matter how remote or silent a wood may be there's always a road or a person within reach: I think of Tennyson when I walk in Gloucestershire, the way that runs through the field, two lovers lately wed, an abbot on an ambling pad. I think as well of old Mrs Whale in her lifetime and Sergeant Wall in his, of Albert the footman at Sezincote, Miss Tavender a schoolmistress, and Joanna Southcott. Blockley Brass Band still performs, weather permitting; there are outings to distant Ramsgate. 'Dubious Dog Contest' the sign outside the British Legion hall announces, and I imagine the pink tongues panting on a Saturday afternoon, setters and spaniels that aren't quite the thing, terriers that should have been Dalmatians. The children of the children who ate the American soldiers' paste sandwiches self-consciously tug the leashes. The sun has brought the hollyhocks out.

The countryside is the setting, but people come first: in spite of disturbance and change it is that that continues, and returning now I feel my childhood instinct was not far wrong. In this warm July, or in their wartime years, in snow or sun, the wolds are unique; and their towns and villages perfectly complement them. Crowded with hastening tourists, all three retain their essence: England is unstifled here.

WILLIAM TREVOR, *Places*

Adlestrop

Yes, I remember Adlestrop –
The name, because one afternoon
Of heat the express-train drew up there
Unwontedly. It was late June.

49

The steam hissed. Someone cleared his throat.
No one left and no one came
On the bare platform. What I saw
Was Adlestrop – only the name.

And willows, willow-herb, and grass,
And meadowsweet, and haycocks dry,
No whit less still and lonely fair
Than the high cloudlets in the sky.

And for a minute a blackbird sang
Close by, and round him, mistier,
Farther and farther, all the birds
Of Oxfordshire and Gloucestershire.

EDWARD THOMAS

Our Village

Our village, that's to say not Miss Mitford's village, but our
    village of Bullock Smithy,
Is come into by an avenue of trees, three oak pollards, two
    elders, and a withy;

And in the middle, there's a green of about not exceeding an
  acre and a half;
It's common to all, and fed off by nineteen cows, six ponies,
  three horses, five asses, two foals, seven pigs, and a calf!
Besides a pond in the middle, as is held by a similar sort of
  common law lease,
And contains twenty ducks, six drakes, three ganders, two
  dead dogs, four drowned kittens, and twelve geese.
Of course the green's cropt very close, and does famous for
  bowling when the little village boys play at cricket;
Only some horse, or pig, or cow, or great jackass, is sure to
  come and stand right before the wicket.
There's fifty-five private houses, let alone barns and
  workshops, and pigstyes, and poultry huts, and such-like
  sheds;
With plenty of public-houses – two Foxes, one Green Man,
  three Bunch of Grapes, one Crown, and six King's Heads.
The Green Man is reckoned the best, as the only one that for
  love or money can raise
A postilion, a blue jacket, two deplorable lame white horses,
  and a ramshackled 'neat postchaise'.
There's one parish church for all the people, whatsoever may
  be their ranks in life or their degrees,
Except one very damp, small, dark, freezing-cold, little
  Methodist chapel of Ease;
And close by the church-yard there's a stone-mason's yard,
  that, when the time is seasonable,
Will furnish with afflictions sore and marble urns and
  cherubims very low and reasonable.
There's a cage, comfortable enough; I've been in it with old
  Jack Jeffrey and Tom Pike;
For the Green Man next door will send you in ale, gin, or
  anything else you like.
I can't speak of the stocks, as nothing remains of them but
  the upright post;
But the pound is kept in repairs for the sake of Cob's horse,
  as is always there almost.
There's a smithy of course, where that queer sort of a chap in
  his way, Old Joe Bradley,
Perpetually hammers and stammers, for he stutters and
  shoes horses very badly.

There's a shop of all sorts, that sells everything, kept by the
widow of Mr Task;
But when you go there, it's ten to one she's out of everything
you ask.
You'll know her house by the swarm of boys, like flies, about
the old sugary cask;
There's another small day-school too, kept by the respectable
Mrs Gaby;
A select establishment, for six little boys and one big, and
four little girls and a baby.
There's a rectory, with pointed gables and strange odd
chimneys that never smokes,
For the rector don't live on his living like other Christian sort
of folks;
There's a barber's, once a week well filled with rough black-
bearded, shock-headed churls,
And a window with two feminine men's heads, and two
masculine ladies in false curls;
There's a butcher's, and a carpenter's, and a plumber's, and a
small greengrocer's and a baker,
But he won't bake on a Sunday, and there's a sexton that's a
coal-merchant besides, and an undertaker;
And a toyshop, but not a whole one, for a village can't
compare with the London shops;
One window sells drums, dolls, kites, carts, bats, Clout's balls,
and the other sells malt and hops.
And Mrs Brown, in domestic economy not to be a bit behind
her betters,
Lets her house to a milliner, a watchmaker, a rat-catcher, a
cobbler, lives in it herself, and it's the post-office for letters.
Now I've gone through all the village – aye, from end to end,
save and except one more house,
But I haven't come to that – and I hope I never shall – and
that's the Village Poor House!

THOMAS HOOD

Notice, for instance, the women who have done their shopping
in the town early in the morning, and are coming home for a
day's work. They are out of breath, and bothered with their
armfuls of purchases; but nine times out of ten their faces look

hopeful; there is no sound of grievance or of worry in their talk; their smiling 'Good-morning' to you proves somehow that it is not a bad morning with them. One day a woman going to the town a little late met another already returning, loaded up with goods. ' 'Ullo, Mrs Fry,' she laughed, 'you be 'bliged to be fust, then?' 'Yes; but I en't bought it *all*; I thought you'd be comin', so I left some for you.' 'That's right of ye. En't it a *nice mornin'*?' 'Jest what we wants! My old man was up an' in he's garden . . .' The words grow indistinguishable as you get farther away; you don't hear what the 'old man' was doing so early, but the country voices sound for a long time, comfortably tuned to the pleasantness of the day.

This sort of thing is so common that I seldom notice it, unless it is varied in some way that attracts attention. For instance, I could not help listening to a woman who was pushing her baby in a perambulator down the hill. The baby sat facing her, as bland as a little image of Buddha, and as unresponsive, but she was chaffing it. 'Well, you *be* a funny little gal, *ben't* ye? Why, you be goin' back'ards into the town! Whoever heared tell o' such a thing – goin' to the town *back*'ards. You *be* a funny little gal!' To me it was a funny little procession, with a touch of the pathetic hidden away in it somewhere; but it bore convincing witness to happiness in at least one home in our valley.

GEORGE BOURNE, *Change in the Village*

The Summer holds: upon its glittering lake
Lie Europe and the islands; many rivers
Wrinkling its surface like a ploughman's palm.
Under the bellies of the grazing horses
On the far side of posts and bridges
The vigorous shadows dwindle; nothing wavers.
Calm at this moment the Dutch sea so shallow
That sunk St Paul's would ever show its golden cross
And still the deep water that divides us still from Norway.
We would show you at first an English village: You shall
    choose its location
Wherever your heart directs you most longingly to look; you
    are loving towards it:

Whether north to Scots Gap and Bellingham where the black
    rams defy the panting engine:
Or west to the Welsh Marches; to the lilting speech and the
    magicians' faces:
Wherever you were a child or had your first affair
There it stands amidst your darling scenery:
A parish bounded by the wreckers' cliff; or meadows where
    browse the Shorthorn and the maplike Frisian
As at Trent Junction where the Soar comes gliding; out of green
    Leicestershire to swell the ampler current.

Hiker with sunburn blisters on your office pallor,
Cross-country champion with corks in your hands,
When you have eaten your sandwich, your salt and your apple,
When you have begged your glass of milk from the ill-kept
    farm,
What is it you see?

I see barns falling, fences broken,
Pasture not ploughland, weeds not wheat.
The great houses remain but only half are inhabited,
Dusty the gunrooms and the stable clocks stationary.
Some have been turned into prep-schools where the diet is in
    the hands of an experienced matron,
Others into club-houses for the golf-bore and the top-hole.
Those who sang in the inns at evening have departed; they saw
    their hope in another country,
Their children have entered the service of the suburban areas;
    they have become typists, mannequins and factory opera-
    tives; they desired a different rhythm of life.
But their places are taken by another population, with views
    about nature,
Brought in charabanc and saloon along arterial roads;
Tourists to whom the Tudor cafés
Offer Bovril and buns upon Breton ware
With leather work as a sideline: Filling stations
Supplying petrol from rustic pumps.
Those who fancy themselves as foxes or desire a special setting
    for spooning
Erect their villas at the right places,
Airtight, lighted, elaborately warmed;

And nervous people who will never marry
Live upon dividends in the old-world cottages
With an animal for friend or a volume of memoirs.

W. H. AUDEN, *The Dog Beneath the Skin*

On the Thames

A cloudy morning when we started, which at first much disappointed me after the splendid evening we had come in by: nevertheless I was in spirits at the idea of getting out of the Cockney waters, and we were scarcely through the lock we had to pass at starting before the sun was out and hot again: the river was nearly new to me really hereabouts and much better than I expected, especially from Chertsey to Staines; it is full of strange character in many places; Laleham, for instance, with its enormous willows and queer suggestions (at any rate) of old houses on the banks: we dined luxuriously on the bank a little below this, and had tea on the grass of Runneymead which (as I remembered) is a most lovely place, on such an afternoon as one can scarcely hope to see again for brightness and clearness. When we had done tea, it became obvious that we should never get to Maidenhead (as we had intended) that night, so after much spilling of wisdom in a discussion of the kind where no one can see any plan but his own as possible, we agreed to make another day of it; Windsor on that night (Wednesday) and Marlow on Thursday. Well, we got to Windsor about eight, and beautiful it was coming into; and with all drawbacks even when one saw it next morning seemed a wonderful place: so we only made 17 miles this day. We all slept in the inn on the waterside: that was Wednesday.

Thursday, Dick took us up to Eton; and again in spite of drawbacks it is yet a glorious place. Once more the morning was grey and even threatening rain (wind N.N.E.), but very soon cleared up again into the brightest of days: a very pleasant morning we had, and dined just above Bray Lock; cook was I, and shut up in the Ark to do the job, appearing like the high-priest at the critical moment pot in hand, – but O the wasps about that osier bed! We got quite used to them at last and by dint of care did not swallow any with our food, nor were stung.

There was a regatta at Maidenhead and both banks crowded

55

with spectators, so that we had to drop the tow-rope before our time, and as the Ark forged slowly along towards the Berkshire side with your servant steering on her roof, and De Morgan labouring at the sculls, you may think that we were chaffed a little. After Maidenhead you go under Cliefden woods, much admired by the world in general; I confess to thinking them rather artificial; also eyeing Mr Dick with reference to their owner I couldn't help thinking of Mr Twemlow and Lord Snigsworthy. But at Cookham Lock how beautiful it was: you get out of the Snigsworthy woods there; the hills fall back from the river, which is very wide there, and you are in the real country, with cows and sheep and farm-houses, the work-a-day world again and not a lacquey's paradise: the country too has plenty of character there, and may even be called beautiful: it was beautiful enough that evening at any rate: the sun had set as we cleared Cookham Lock, and we went facing the west, which was cloudless and golden, till it got quite dark: by that same dark we had to get through the Marlow Lock, with no little trouble, as we had to skirt a huge weir which roared so that we couldn't hear each other speak, and so to our night's lodging: Crom and I in the Ark close to the roaring weir, Dick and De M. in the inn (a noisy one) and the ladies up town, over the bridge. We took them there, and as we left the little house, looked up the street, and saw the streamers of the Northern Lights flickering all across that part of the sky, just as I saw them in '71 (and not since) in the harbour of Thorshaven: it was very mysterious and almost frightening to see them over the summer leafage so unexpectedly in a place I at least had not seen by daylight.

WILLIAM MORRIS, *Letters*, 1880

A canal in a pastoral setting, with trees bordering its edges and the water full of blue sky, is a very beautiful thing. But a canal set among the mournful industrial towns of the Midlands can give one strange shocks of pleasure; its life and beauty lie in its reflections. When these cannot be seen, when the water is ruffled by wind and rain, it is as though a blind had been drawn down; the canal is dead. I shall never forget some of the reflections I have seen. One was astonishingly dramatic, amid its dismal surroundings.

At one point the canal to Wolverhampton runs very close to a reservoir in the centre of Birmingham. On a wedge of land there showmen of the last century, with great energy and a modicum of taste, had built an amusement park.

When I saw it, almost everything was in a state of decay. Over a wreck of faded plaster, which had been the main entrance, broken electric light bulbs swung from painted arches. Mud and black water, settling under a hut of cheap colours, oozed beneath the fences of the main enclosure. Inside it, large tarpaulin-covered shapes showed where once amusement booths, calliopes and heaving dragons had carried on a busy trade. Now everything stood silent, a picture of neglect.

Here the canal is wide and an old timber jetty, leaning lopsidedly, is built out into the water. Rushes grow beneath it, the tallest leaves filling the gaps where the floorboards should be. It was from the end of this jetty that I saw the reflection of a circle of wooden horses under a gay roofing.

Each horse was poised in a frozen gallop on a twisted barley-sugar pillar. Some were gilded, others white, dapple-grey or black. All had painted on them flowers and baroque harness, such as circus ponies wear. One horse was spotted all over with the sort of flowers you see painted on the sides of a monkey boat; full, bulbous blooms growing fanwise on spiky stems from a central spray.

In the gleaming dark-green water the colour of the horses was subdued and the gilded shapes looked warm against a leaden sky. A cloud moved away from the sun and the reflected tarpaulins and chimneys glistened in the April light. Looking up, I could see between the horses and the swaying canopy the gilded dome of the Town Hall, trying in vain to make the Midland capital imposing. The whole scene was a strange patch of enchantment in a forgotten backwater.

Another reflection I remember vividly showed the industrial canal in its grimmest mood. The place was a waterway which runs from east to west near the heart of Birmingham. There is a cutting there which is bordered at first by dull red houses. Farther on it develops into a deep, wet, brick-faced excavation, passing down a succession of locks, deeper and deeper into the shadows of tall offices and factories, with dripping walls and trampled towpath. Halfway down this weeping gully, in a puddle of water on the towpath, I saw a brilliant white cloud in blue sky, while all around was dark green and stormy. The bright cloud seemed to hold a promise of the sunny, peaceful, lazy countryside which lay beyond the city.

Another reflection which I associate with the Midlands in sleepy mood was in clear water, which showed a replica of a boat, every detail complete, against a luminous sky. Behind it was the half-circle of a humped bridge with each stone perfectly repeated in the water. Tall elms lay black in the canal behind the bridge. This scene, with a quiet sky of clouds resting on each other, struck me as very typical of the middle counties in their most pleasant mood.

JOHN O'CONNOR, *Canals, Barges and People*

The Rolling English Road

Before the Roman came to Rye or out to Severn strode,
The rolling English drunkard made the rolling English road.
A reeling road, a rolling road, that rambles round the shire,
And after him the parson ran, the sexton and the squire;
A merry road, a mazy road, and such as we did tread
The night we went to Birmingham by way of Beachy Head.

I knew no harm of Bonaparte and plenty of the Squire,
And for to fight the Frenchman I did not much desire;
But I did bash their baggonets because they came arrayed
To straighten out the crooked road an English drunkard made,
Where you and I went down the lane with ale-mugs in our
    hands,
The night we went to Glastonbury by way of Goodwin Sands.

His sins they were forgiven him; or why do flowers run
Behind him; and the hedges all strengthening in the sun?
The wild thing went from left to right and knew not which was
    which,
But the wild rose was above him when they found him in the
    ditch.
God pardon us, nor harden us; we did not see so clear
The night we went to Bannockburn by way of Brighton Pier.

My friends, we will not go again or ape an ancient rage,
Or stretch the folly of our youth to be the shame of age,
But walk with clearer eyes and ears this path that wandereth,
And see undrugged in evening light the decent inn of death;
For there is good news yet to hear and fine things to be seen,
Before we go to Paradise by way of Kensal Green.

G. K. CHESTERTON

From Cambridge to St Ives the land is generally in open, unfenced fields, and some common fields; generally stiff land, and some of it not very good, and wheat, in many places, looking rather thin. From St Ives to Chateris (which last is in the Isle of Ely), the land is better, particularly as you approach the latter place. From Chateris I came back to Huntingdon, and once more saw its beautiful meadows, of which I spoke when I went thither in 1823. From Huntingdon, through Stilton, to Stamford (the last two in Lincolnshire) is a country of rich arable land and grass fields, and of beautiful meadows. The enclosures are very large, the soil red, with a whitish stone below; very much like the soil at and near Ross in Herefordshire, and like that near Coventry and Warwick. Here, as all over this country, everlasting fine sheep. The houses all along here are built of the stone of the county: you seldom see brick. The churches are large, lofty, and fine, and give proof that the country was formerly much more populous than it is now, and that the people had a vast deal more of wealth in their hands, and at their own disposal. There are three beautiful churches at Stamford, not less, I dare say, than three (*quaere*) hundred years old; but two of them (I did not go to the other) are as perfect as when just finished, except as to the *images*, most of which have been destroyed by the ungrateful Protestant barbarians, of different sorts, but some of which (*out of reach* of their ruthless hands) are still in the niches.

From Stamford to Peterborough is a country of the same description, with the additional beauty of woods here and there, and with meadows just like those at Huntingdon, and not surpassed by those on the Severn near Worcester nor by those on the Avon at Tewkesbury. The cathedral at Peterborough is exquisitely beautiful, and I have great pleasure in saying that, contrary to the *more magnificent* pile at Ely, it is kept in good order; the Bishop (Herbert Marsh) residing a good deal on the spot; and though he *did* write a pamphlet to justify and urge on the war, the ruinous war, and though he *did* get a *pension* for it, he is, they told me, very good to the poor people. My daughters had a great desire to see, and I had a great desire they should see, the burial place of that ill-used, that savagely-treated woman, and that honour to woman-kind, Catherine, queen of the ferocious tyrant, Henry the Eighth. To the infamy of that ruffian, and the shame of after ages, there is no *monument* to record her virtues and her sufferings; and the remains of this daughter of the wise Ferdinand and of the generous Isabella, who sold her jewels to enable Columbus to discover the New World, lie under the floor of the cathedral, commemorated by a short inscription on a plate of brass. All men, Protestants or not Protestants, feel as I feel on this subject; search the *hearts* of the bishop and of his dean and chapter, and these feelings are there; but to do *justice* to the memory of this illustrious victim of tyranny, would be to cast a reflection on that event, to which they owe their rich possessions, and, at the same time, to suggest ideas not very favourable to the descendants of those who divided amongst them the plunder of the people arising out of that event, and which descendants are their patrons, and give them what they possess. From this cause, and no other, it is that the memory of the virtuous Catherine is unblazoned, while that of the tyrannic, the cruel, and the immoral Elizabeth, is recorded with all possible veneration, and all possible varnishing over of her disgusting amours and endless crimes.

WILLIAM COBBETT, *Rural Rides*

There is no better way to plunge *in medias res*, for the stranger who wishes to know something of England, than to spend a fortnight in Warwickshire. It is the core and centre of the English world: midmost England, unmitigated England.

HENRY JAMES, *English Hours*

On the 7th we passed through Stamford and Grantham, and dined at Newark, where I had only time to observe that the market-place was uncommonly spacious and neat. In London we should call it a square, though the sides were neither straight nor parallel. We came, at night, to Doncaster, and went to church in the morning, where Chambers found the monument of Robert of Doncaster, who says on his stone something like this:– What I gave, that I have; what I spent, that I had; what I left, that I lost. – So saith Robert of Doncaster, who reigned in the world sixty-seven years, and all that time lived not one. Here we were invited to dinner, and therefore made no great haste away.

We reached York however that night; I was much disordered with old complaints. Next morning we saw the Minster, an edifice of loftiness and elegance equal to the highest hopes of architecture. I remember nothing but the dome of St Paul's that can be compared with the middle walk. The Chapterhouse is a circular building, very stately, but I think excelled by the Chapterhouse of Lincoln.

I then went to see the ruins of the Abbey, which are almost vanished, and I remember nothing of them distinct.

The next visit was to the jail, which they call the castle; a fabrick built lately, such is terrestrial mutability, out of the materials of the ruined Abbey. The under jailor was very officious to show his fetters, in which there was no contrivance. The head jailor came in, and seeing me look I supposed fatigued, offered me wine, and when I went away would not suffer his servant to take money. The jail is accounted the best in the kingdom, and you find the jailor deserving of his dignity.

We dined at York, and went on to Northallerton, a place of which I know nothing, but that it afforded us a lodging on Monday night, and about two hundred and seventy years ago gave birth to Roger Ascham.

Next morning we changed our horses at Darlington, where Mr Cornelius Harrison, a cousin-german of mine, was perpetual curate. He was the only one of my relations who ever rose in fortune above penury, or in character above neglect.

The church is built crosswise, with a fine spire, and might invite a traveller to survey it, but I perhaps wanted vigour, and thought I wanted time.

The next stage brought us to Durham, a place of which Mr Thrale bade me take particular notice. The bishop's palace has the appearance of an old feudal castle, built upon an eminence, and looking down upon the river, upon which was formerly thrown a drawbridge, as I suppose to be raised at night, lest the Scots should pass it.

The cathedral has a massyness and solidity such as I have seen in no other place; it rather awes than pleases, as it strikes with a kind of gigantick dignity, and aspires to no other praise than that of rocky solidity and indeterminate duration. I had none of my friends resident, and therefore saw but little. The library is mean and scanty.

At Durham, beside all expectation, I met an old friend: Miss Fordyce is married there to a physician. We met, I think, with honest kindness on both sides. I thought her much decayed, and having since heard that the banker had involved her husband in his extensive ruin, I cannot forbear to think that I saw in her withered features more impression of sorrow than of time . . .

He that wanders about the world sees new forms of human misery, and if he chances to meet an old friend, meets a face darkened with troubles.

SAMUEL JOHNSON, letter to Mrs Thrale, 12 August 1773

62

Here

Swerving east, from rich industrial shadows
And traffic all night north; swerving through fields
Too thin and thistled to be called meadows,
And now and then a harsh-named halt, that shields
Workmen at dawn; swerving to solitude
Of skies and scarecrows, haystacks, hares and pheasants,
And the widening river's slow presence,
The piled gold clouds, the shining gull-marked mud,

Gathers to the surprise of a large town:
Here domes and statues, spires and cranes cluster
Beside grain-scattered streets, barge-crowded water,
And residents from raw estates, brought down
The dead straight miles by stealing flat-faced trolleys,
Push through plate-glass swing doors to their desires –
Cheap suits, red kitchen-ware, sharp shoes, iced lollies,
Electric mixers, toasters, washers, driers –

A cut-price crowd, urban yet simple, dwelling
Where only salesmen and relations come
Within a terminate and fishy-smelling
Pastoral of ships up streets, the slave museum,
Tattoo-shops, consulates, grim head-scarfed wives;
And out beyond its mortgaged half-built edges
Fast-shadowed wheat-fields, running high as hedges,
Isolate villages, where removed lives

Loneliness clarifies. Here silence stands
Like heat. Here leaves unnoticed thicken,
Hidden weeds flower, neglected waters quicken,
Luminously-peopled air ascends;
And past the poppies bluish neutral distance
Ends the land suddenly beyond a beach
Of shapes and shingle. Here is unfenced existence:
Facing the sun, untalkative, out of reach.

PHILIP LARKIN

63

Everywhere we walked buildings were either going up or coming down, or else the roads were being widened to take yet more motor-cars. An endless process of construction and destruction. It seemed there was neither time nor room for pedestrians. We were literally a dying breed. At one moment we trotted single file, cowering away from the traffic, along a ribbon of pavement beside a motorway, with something like the Berlin Wall towering above us. A sign on the roof said it was the Birmingham School of Music; I hope they'd remembered to sound-proof it. Then we escaped into a little lane in which rank alder and dirty privet grew. To the right a thirty-storey building, and another even higher to the left, the two joined by a labyrinth of subterranean passages and overhead tunnels. Through a gap in the concrete I could see a golden dome, and the thin spire of an old, blackened church. We ran along a cat-walk called Paradise Place; some wit had scrawled underneath, 'And chips'. We had lunch in a noisy pub beneath an Insurance block. Plastic grapes hung from the ceiling and there were hundreds of people, sweating and laughing and knocking back the beer as though they were on holiday in some Mediterranean resort. Everyone merry as crickets, and hungry; plates heaped with salad and sausages, chips and tinned salmon and scotch eggs, cheeses and hunks of french bread spread with onion rings and chutney. Nobody glanced at the nightmare outside, the windows framed in purple grapes. What must it be like in winter when the rain sweeps down and the wind blows the refuse through the concrete tunnels? Do people hurl themselves from the office blocks and the fly-overs into the dangerous streets below?

By car to look at Spaghetti Junction – almost a tourist attraction – along Perry Barr High Street with its pre-war villas cast up at the edge of a motorway wide enough for a procession of May Day tanks, and a crematorium to the right with a poster flapping on the gates, 'Put Yourself in Our Place.' In spite of the mess, the dug-up drains, the overhead cables, the petrol stations and the demolition sites they were building three-storey desirable homes at the side of the fume-ridden road.

We came to a housing estate caught between the hell behind and the anarchy ahead. The road sloped down beside poplars and petered out in fields straddled with high-rise flats and giant pylons. What a view for the airborne tenants. From this angle the Junction was a child's switchback track propped on toy bricks. To get closer to it we drove along a winding lane miraculously dolloped with horse dung, and into Meadow Avenue, past a black girl wearing a black frock with a white collar, prancing on high heels into a dress shop called Lo-Cost. Beyond the avenue lay no-man's-land: nothing but the pylons holding hands as they marched to the horizon, and a railway line under a cat's cradle of rusty gantries jammed into the ruined earth.

Trust House Forte, with an unerring eye for beauty, had built an hotel on the slope up to the Junction. It had its own flag-poles and hot-air chimneys and stood on a plateau of stained and splitting concrete, stunted saplings ringed in wire netting bursting through the cracks in the forecourt. Fancy having to book to stay there. Then the road climbed higher, and round, and up again, and then, looping a suicide loop, we skidded into a tunnel, ahead of a container lorry and behind a transporter shuddering under a load of new Metro motor-cars, and emerged into a six-lane roar of barbarous traffic racing beneath the darkening sky.

Believe it or not, down below to our left in the shadows of the support blocks, people were fishing on a man-made lake.

BERYL BAINBRIDGE, *English Journey*

The real tragedy of England, as I see it, is the tragedy of ugli-ness. The country is so lovely; the man-made England so vile.

D. H. LAWRENCE

*Lines Composed a Few Miles above Tintern Abbey,
on Revisiting the Banks of the Wye during a Tour. 13 July 1798*

Five years have past; five summers, with the length
Of five long winters! and again I hear
These waters, rolling from their mountain-springs
With a soft inland murmur. – Once again
Do I behold these steep and lofty cliffs,

That on a wild secluded scene impress
Thoughts of more deep seclusion; and connect
The landscape with the quiet of the sky.
The day is come when I again repose
Here, under this dark sycamore, and view
These plots of cottage-ground, these orchard-tufts,
Which at this season, with their unripe fruits,
Are clad in one green hue, and lose themselves
'Mid groves and copses. Once again I see
These hedge-rows, hardly hedge-rows, little lines
Of sportive wood run wild: these pastoral farms,
Green to the very door; and wreaths of smoke
Sent up, in silence, from among the trees!
With some uncertain notice, as might seem
Of vagrant dwellers in the houseless woods,
Or of some Hermit's cave, where by his fire
The Hermit sits alone.
                              These beauteous forms,
Through a long absence, have not been to me
As is a landscape to a blind man's eye:
But oft, in lonely rooms, and 'mid the din
Of towns and cities, I have owed to them,
In hours of weariness, sensations sweet,
Felt in the blood, and felt along the heart;
And passing even into my purer mind,
With tranquil restoration: – feelings too
Of unremembered pleasure: such, perhaps,
As have no slight or trivial influence
On that best portion of a good man's life,
His little, nameless, unremembered, acts
Of kindness and of love. Nor less, I trust,
To them I may have owed another gift,
Of aspect more sublime; that blessed mood,
In which the burthen of the mystery,
In which the heavy and the weary weight
Of all this unintelligible world,
Is lightened: – that serene and blessed mood,
In which the affections gently lead us on, –
Until, the breath of this corporeal frame
And even the motion of our human blood
Almost suspended, we are laid asleep

In body, and become a living soul:
While with an eye made quiet by the power
Of harmony, and the deep power of joy,
We see into the life of things.
                                    If this
Be but a vain belief, yet, oh! how oft –
In darkness and amid the many shapes
Of joyless daylight; when the fretful stir
Unprofitable, and the fever of the world,
Have hung upon the beatings of my heart –
How oft, in spirit, have I turned to thee,
O sylvan Wye! thou wanderer thro' the woods,
How often has my spirit turned to thee!

And now, with gleams of half-extinguished thought,
With many recognitions dim and faint,
And somewhat of a sad perplexity,
The picture of the mind revives again:
While here I stand, not only with the sense
Of present pleasure, but with pleasing thoughts
That in this moment there is life and food
For future years. And so I dare to hope,
Though changed, no doubt, from what I was when first
I came among these hills; when like a roe
I bounded o'er the mountains, by the sides
Of the deep rivers, and the lonely streams,
Wherever nature led: more like a man
Flying from something that he dreads than one
Who sought the thing he loved. For nature then
(The coarser pleasures of my boyish days,
And their glad animal movements all gone by)
To me was all in all. – I cannot paint
What then I was. The sounding cataract
Haunted me like a passion: the tall rock,
The mountain, and the deep and gloomy wood,
Their colours and their forms, were then to me
An appetite; a feeling and a love,
That had no need of a remoter charm,
By thought supplied, nor any interest
Unborrowed from the eye. – That time is past,
And all its aching joys are now no more,

And all its dizzy raptures. Not for this
Faint I, nor mourn nor murmur; other gifts
Have followed; for such loss, I would believe,
Abundant recompense. For I have learned
To look on nature, not as in the hour
Of thoughtless youth; but hearing oftentimes
The still, sad music of humanity,
Nor harsh nor grating, though of ample power
To chasten and subdue. And I have felt
A presence that disturbs me with the joy
Of elevated thoughts; a sense sublime
Of something far more deeply interfused,
Whose dwelling is the light of setting suns,
And the round ocean and the living air,
And the blue sky, and in the mind of man:
A motion and a spirit, that impels
All thinking things, all objects of all thought,
And rolls through all things. Therefore am I still
A lover of the meadows and the woods,
And mountains; and of all that we behold
From this green earth; of all the mighty world
Of eye, and ear, – both what they half create,
And what perceive; well pleased to recognize
In nature and the language of the sense
The anchor of my purest thoughts, the nurse,
The guide, the guardian of my heart, and soul
Of all my moral being.
                                        Nor perchance,
If I were not thus taught, should I the more
Suffer my genial spirits to decay:
For thou art with me here upon the banks
Of this fair river; thou my dearest Friend,
My dear, dear Friend; and in thy voice I catch
The language of my former heart, and read
My former pleasures in the shooting lights
Of thy wild eyes. Oh! yet a little while
May I behold in thee what I was once,
My dear, dear Sister! and this prayer I make,
Knowing that Nature never did betray
The heart that loved her; 'tis her privilege,
Through all the years of this our life, to lead

From joy to joy: for she can so inform
The mind that is within us, so impress
With quietness and beauty, and so feed
With lofty thoughts, that neither evil tongues,
Rash judgments, nor the sneers of selfish men,
Nor greetings where no kindness is, nor all
The dreary intercourse of daily life,
Shall e'er prevail against us, or disturb
Our cheerful faith, that all which we behold
Is full of blessings. Therefore let the moon
Shine on thee in thy solitary walk;
And let the misty mountain-winds be free
To blow against thee: and, in after years,
When these wild ecstasies shall be matured
Into a sober pleasure; when thy mind
Shall be a mansion for all lovely forms,
Thy memory be as a dwelling-place
For all sweet sounds and harmonies; oh! then,
If solitude, or fear, or pain, or grief,
Should be thy portion, with what healing thoughts
Of tender joy wilt thou remember me,
And these my exhortations! Nor, perchance –
If I should be where I no more can hear
Thy voice, nor catch from thy wild eyes these gleams
Of past existence – wilt thou then forget
That on the banks of this delightful stream
We stood together; and that I, so long
A worshipper of Nature, hither came
Unwearied in that service: rather say
With warmer love – oh! with far deeper zeal
Of holier love. Nor wilt thou then forget
That after many wanderings, many years
Of absence, these steep woods and lofty cliffs,
And this green pastoral landscape, were to me
More dear, both for themselves and for thy sake.

WILLIAM WORDSWORTH

THE ENGLISH
CHARACTER

It is worth trying for a moment to put oneself in the position of a foreign observer, new to England, but unprejudiced, and able because of his work to keep in touch with ordinary, useful, unspectacular people. . . . Almost certainly he would find the salient characteristics of the English common people to be artistic insensibility, gentleness, respect for legality, suspicion of foreigners, sentimentality about animals, hypocrisy, exaggerated class distinctions, and an obsession with sport.

Our imaginary observer would certainly be struck by our gentleness: by the orderly behaviour of English crowds, the lack of pushing and quarrelling, the willingness to form queues, the good temper of harassed, overworked people like bus conductors. The manners of the English working class are not always very graceful, but they are extremely considerate. Great care is taken in showing a stranger the way, blind people can travel across London with the certainty that they will be helped on and off every bus and across every street.

The English people are not good haters, their memory is very short, their patriotism is largely unconscious, they have no love of military glory and not much admiration for great men. They have the virtues and the vices of an old-fashioned people. To twentieth-century political theories they oppose not another theory of their own, but a moral quality which must be vaguely described as decency. On the day in 1936 when the Germans reoccupied the Rhineland I was in a northern mining town. I happened to go into a pub just after this piece of news, which quite obviously meant war, had come over the wireless, and I remarked to the others at the bar, 'The German army has crossed the Rhine.' With a vague air of capping a quotation someone answered, 'Parley-voo.' No more response than that! Nothing will ever wake these people up, I thought. But later in

the evening, at the same pub, someone sang a song which had
recently come out, with the chorus –

> For you can't do that there 'ere,
> No, you can't do that there 'ere;
> Anywhere else you can do that there,
> But you can't do that there 'ere!

And it struck me that perhaps this was the English answer to
fascism. At any rate it is true that it has not happened here, in
spite of fairly favourable circumstances. The amount of liberty,
intellectual or other, that we enjoy in England ought not to be
exaggerated, but the fact that it did not markedly diminish in
nearly six years of desperate war is a hopeful symptom.

GEORGE ORWELL, *The English People*

I can conceive of no one more objectionable than the authentic
Englishman. He is like a sheep with a sheep's practical instinct
for sniffing out its food in the field. But the beauty of the field
and the sky above is beyond his perception.

RICHARD WAGNER

The English may not like music; but they absolutely love the
noise it makes.

SIR THOMAS BEECHAM

I do not know how it is, but whenever I consider this English
society, always, beyond the human head and the splendid
torso, I find myself aware of the bestial and muck-fouled hind-
quarters.

HIPPOLYTE TAINE, *Notes on England*

My hope of an Englishman is limited. You might perhaps get
him to give up his Toryism and his Radicalism, he may even
abandon his Protestantism, his Dissent or his Church of England, but his frock coat never: he'll hold to his respectability to

his dying day – the way he must put on a coat over all the rest of his clothes to go out for a walk in on a Sunday is inborn in him.

EDWARD BURNE-JONES

To think is no part of their character. Instead of thoughts, the English have traditions.

The tradition of the Home, for instance.

Even the French – a volatile and irreverent race, with no marked bias in favour of Albion – have preferred not to translate this word, but to recognize it as unalterably English in origin and spirit by referring to it as 'le home'.

Yet how do the English treat 'le home' – that is, theoretically and traditionally, the backbone of their country?

Their first care is to remove their children from it by sending them to boarding-school almost as soon as they can walk, and keeping them there until they are old enough to be sent still farther away.

Their next is to avoid the proximity of their relations. Unlike the Latin races, the English seldom keep a widowed mother-in-law, an unmarried sister and a couple of canaries on the top floor, an asthmatic uncle and his housekeeper on the third, and a centenarian cousin in a little room behind the kitchen.

They speak, write and sing of Home Sweet Home, and by this means have built up the tradition that it is a thoroughly English institution. Once tradition is firmly established, the thing is done.

The danger of having to think is practically eliminated.

Another tradition that is rooted not only in our own soil, but in the minds of the rest of the world, is the devotion of the English to animals. Certainly, they will speak affectionately to and of their dogs and horses, which is more than they will do concerning their friends and family – but between the dogs and horses and the rest of the brute creation a sharp line has been drawn. The fox, the deer, the badger, the otter, the pheasant, and many others would have but little to say in praise of the animal-loving English, were they consulted. Even the domestic cat is, for the most part, only viewed as an inferior kind of dog, its sole virtue being that it will – like its owners – kill other, smaller animals.

But by dint of never thinking about it, the English firmly believe themselves to be the only nation on earth that is really kind to its animals.

Indeed, the power of self-delusion possessed by our singular race is almost phenomenal, the more so because it cannot be called the product of imagination, for the English neither possess, nor wish to possess, any imagination at all. They only possess, to a very high degree, the quality of faith as defined by the schoolboy: Believing what you know to be untrue.

A very brief list of such beliefs comes to one's mind almost automatically. Most Englishmen, if forced into analysing their own creeds – which Heaven forbid – are convinced that God is an Englishman – probably educated at Eton.

That all good women are naturally frigid.

That any change in the British Constitution would be for the worse.

That England is going to rack and ruin.

That England is the finest country in the world.

That all foreigners are slightly mad.

That any one disagreeing on any of these points ought to be shot.

The beliefs of Englishwomen are confined to the more domestic problems of life.

That all men are just like children.

That it is better to be dowdy than smart.

That listening to the wireless is meritorious but reading a novel is waste of time.

That a Sale is a place where goods can be obtained for less money than they are really worth.

That children are a blessing to their parents.

Enough has now perhaps been said to show that the English, whatever else they may be, are agreeably inconsistent. (Unfortunately, it was an American who first wrote: Dare to be inconsistent.)

E. M. DELAFIELD, Introduction to *The British Character* by Pont

Every Englishman runs to *The Times* with his little grievances, as a child runs to his mother.

NATHANIEL HAWTHORNE

Life in England is not cheerful, but it is interesting.

IVAN TURGENEV

It is Bank Holiday today, and the streets are overcrowded with swarms of people. Never is so clearly to be seen the vulgarity of the people as at these holiday times. Their notion of a holiday is to rush in crowds to some sweltering place, such as the Crystal Palace, and there sit and drink and quarrel themselves into stupidity. Miserable children are lugged about, yelling at the top of their voices, and are beaten because they yell. Troops of hideous creatures drive wildly about the town in gigs, donkey-carts, cabbage-carts, dirt-carts, and think it enjoyment. The pleasure of peace and quietness, of rest for body and mind, is not understood. Thousands are tempted by cheap trips to go off for the day to the seaside, and succeed in wearying themselves to death, for the sake of eating a greasy meal in a Margate Coffee-shop, and getting five minutes' glimpse of the sea through eyes blinded with dirt and perspiration. Places like Hampstead Heath and the various parks and commons are packed with screeching drunkards, one general mass of dust and heat and rage and exhaustion. Yet this is the best kind of holiday the people are capable of.

It is utterly absurd, this idea of setting aside single days for great public holidays. It will never do anything but harm. What we want is a general shortening of working hours all the year round, so that, for instance, all labour would be over at 4 o'clock in the afternoon. Then the idea of hours of leisure would become familiar to the people and they would learn to make some sensible use of them. Of course this is impossible so long as we work for working's sake. All the world's work – all that is really necessary for the health and comfort and even luxury of mankind – could be performed in three or four hours of each day. There is so much labour just because there is so much money-grubbing. Every man has to fight for a living with his neighbour, and the grocer who keeps his shop open till half an hour after midnight has an advantage over him who closes at twelve. Work in itself is *not an end; only a means;* but we nowadays make it an end, and three-fourths of the world cannot understand anything else.

GEORGE GISSING, *Letters*, 1882

Let us pause to consider the English,
Who when they pause to consider themselves they get all
    reticently thrilled and tinglish,
Because every Englishman is convinced of one thing, viz:
That to be an Englishman is to belong to the most exclusive
    club there is:
A club to which benighted bounders of Frenchmen and
    Germans and Italians et cetera cannot even aspire to belong,
Because they don't even speak English, and the Americans are
    worst of all because they speak it wrong. . . .

OGDEN NASH

When you look at England, you see enviable suburbs and unique provincial towns and a little green countryside. But soon you don't notice all that because the English themselves seize your attention and won't let it go. I have dreamed of the English as such, in a mass, advancing towards me like creatures in *Alice in Wonderland* – snooty and snobby, fascinating in their social stances, often as cold as crystal. Some are on horseback, others trail dogs on chains or cosset little cats or canaries, for the English often seem edgy if not in the presence of an animal. For the stranger, the warmth comes later: when they accept the stranger, they cosset him, too, and their friendliness knows no bounds. They have rules and taboos, to be taught to animal and stranger, rules that go deeper and mean more than the conventions of the Continentals or the Americans. England is a complex nation. And it contains great freedom: that should never be forgotten.

WILLIAM TREVOR

Sound English commonsense – the inherited stupidity of the race.

OSCAR WILDE

Few people realize the tomblike silence in which most Englishmen spend their lives. Their education trains to silence, their marriage system encourages it, their belief in physical exercise makes intellectual silence easy.

HUGH WALPOLE

Lord Hartington

He could not understand why it was; but whenever there was a dispute about cards in a club, it was brought to *him* to settle. It was most odd. But it was true. In public affairs, no less than in private, Lord Hartington's decisions carried an extraordinary weight. The feeling of his idle friends in high society was shared by the great mass of the English people; here was a man they could trust. For indeed he was built upon a pattern which was very dear to his countrymen. It was not simply that he was honest: it was that his honesty was an English honesty – an honesty which naturally belonged to one who, so it seemed to them, was the living image of what an Englishman should be. In Lord Hartington they saw, embodied and glorified, the very qualities which were nearest to their hearts – impartiality, solidity, common sense – the qualities by which they themselves longed to be distinguished, and by which, in their happier moments, they believed they were. If ever they began to have misgivings, there, at any rate, was the example of Lord Hartington to guide them – Lord Hartington who was never self-seeking, who was never excited, and who had no imagination at all. Everything they knew about him fitted into the picture, adding to their admiration and respect. His fondness for field sports gave them a feeling of security; and certainly there could be no nonsense about a man who confessed to two ambitions – to become Prime Minister and to win the Derby – and who put the second above the first. They loved him for his casualness – for his inexactness – for refusing to make life a cut-and-dried business – for ramming an official despatch of high importance into his coat-pocket, and finding it there, still unopened, at Newmarket, several days later. They loved him for his hatred of fine sentiments; they were delighted when they heard that at some function, on a florid speaker's avowing that 'this was the proudest moment of his life', Lord Hartington had growled in an undertone 'the proudest moment of *my* life was when my pig won the prize at Skipton fair'. Above all, they loved him for being dull. It was the greatest comfort – with Lord Hartington they could always be absolutely certain that he would never, in any circumstances, be either brilliant, or subtle, or surprising, or impassioned, or profound. As they sat, listening to his speeches, in which considerations of stolid plainness succeeded one another with complete flatness, they felt, involved and supported by the colossal tedium, that their confidence was finally assured. They looked up, and took their fill of the sturdy obvious presence. The inheritor of a splendid dukedom might almost have passed for a farm hand. Almost, but not quite. For an air, that was difficult to explain, of preponderating authority lurked in the solid figure; and the lordly breeding of the House of Cavendish was visible in the large, long, bearded, unimpressionable face.

LYTTON STRACHEY, *Eminent Victorians*

In France it is rude to let a conversation drop; in England it is rash to keep it up. No one there will blame you for silence. When you have not opened your mouth for three years, they will think, 'This Frenchman is a nice quiet fellow.'

ANDRÉ MAUROIS, *Three Letters on the English*

Once, on coming from the Continent, almost the first inscription I saw in my native English was this: 'To let, a Genteel House, up this road.' And it struck me forcibly, for I had not come across the idea of gentility, among the upper limestone of the Alps, for seven months; nor do I think that the Continental nations in general have the idea. They would have advertised a 'pretty' house, or a 'large' one, or a 'convenient' one; but they could not by any use of the terms afforded by their several languages have got at the English 'genteel'. Consider, a little, all the meanness that there is in that epithet . . .

JOHN RUSKIN, Modern Painters

I have travelled much, and seen many men and cities; and, in truth, I think that our country of England produces the best soldiers, sailors, razors, tailors, brewers, hatters, and rogues, of all. Especially there is no cheat like an English cheat. Our society produces them in the greatest numbers as well as of the greatest excellence. We supply all Europe with them. I defy you to point out a great city of the Continent where half a dozen of them are not to be found: proofs of our enterprise and samples of our home manufacture. Try Rome, Cheltenham, Baden, Toeplitz, Madrid, or Tzarskoselo: I have been in every one of them, and give you my honour that the Englishman is the best rascal to be found in all; better than your eager Frenchman; your swaggering Irishman, with a red velvet waistcoat and red whiskers; your grave Spaniard, with horrid goggle eyes and profuse diamond shirt-pins; your tallow-faced German baron, with white moustaches and double chin, fat, pudgy, dirty fingers, and great gold thumb-ring; better even than your nondescript Russian – swindler and spy as he is by loyalty and education – the most dangerous antagonist we have.

WILLIAM MAKEPEACE THACKERAY, Character Sketches

The English are the only people in the world habitually guilty of the discourtesy of sending letters abroad insufficiently stamped. It comes of their impatience of detail.

GEORGE GISSING, Commonplace Book

Self-love is the great malady of England.

ELIZABETH BARRETT BROWNING

The English are so Nice!

The English are so nice
so awfully nice
they are the nicest people in the world.

And what's more, they're very nice about being nice
about your being nice as well!
If you're not nice they soon make you feel it.

Americans and French and Germans and so on
they're all very well
but they're not *really* nice, you know.
They're not nice in *our* sense of the word, are they now?

That's why one doesn't have to take them seriously.
We must be nice to them, of course,
of course, naturally.
But it doesn't really matter when you say to them,
they don't really understand
you can just say anything to them:
be nice, you know, just nice
but you must never take them seriously, they wouldn't
    understand,
just be nice, you know! oh, fairly nice,
not too nice of course, they take advantage
but nice enough, just nice enough
to let them feel they're not quite as nice as they might be.

D. H. LAWRENCE

The most remarkable thing I have observed since I came abroad is that there are no people so obviously mad as the English. The French, the Italians, have great follies, great faults, but then they are so national that they cease to be striking. In England, tempers vary so excessively, that almost everyone's faults are peculiar to himself. I take this diversity to proceed partly from our climate, partly from our government; the first is changeable and makes us queer, the latter permits our queerness to operate as they please. If one could avoid contracting this queerness, it must certainly be the most entertaining to live in England, where such a variety of incidents continually amuse.

HORACE WALPOLE

Public Schools

I should like to know . . . how much ruin has been caused by that accursed system which is called in England 'the education of a gentleman'. Go, my son, for ten years to a public school, that 'world in miniature'; learn 'to fight for yourself' against the time that your real struggles shall begin. Begin to be selfish at ten years of age; study for another ten years; get a competent knowledge of boxing, swimming, rowing, and cricket, with a pretty knack of Latin hexameters and a decent smattering of Greek plays – do this and a fond father shall bless you – bless the two thousand pounds which he has spent in acquiring all these benefits for you. And, besides, what else have you not learned? You have been many hundreds of times to chapel, and have learned to consider the religious service performed there as the vainest parade in the world. If your father is a grocer, you have been beaten for his sake, and have learned to be ashamed of him. You have learned to forget (as how should you remember, being separated from them for three-fourths of your time?) ties and natural affections of home. You have learned, if you have a kindly heart and an open hand, to compete with associates much more wealthy than yourself; and to consider money as not much, but honour – the honour of dining and consorting with your betters – as a great deal. All this does the public-school and college boy learn; and woe be to his knowledge! Alas! what natural tenderness and kindly clinging filial affection is he taught to trample on and despise!

WILLIAM MAKEPEACE THACKERAY, *A Shabby Genteel Story*

The English do not know what to think until they are coached, laboriously and insistently for years, in the proper and becoming opinion.

GEORGE BERNARD SHAW

There is nothing which an Englishman enjoys more than the pleasure of sulkiness – of not being forced to hear a word from anybody which may occasion to him the necessity of replying. It is not so much that Mr Bull disdains the talk, as that Mr Bull has nothing to say. His forefathers have been out of spirits for six or seven hundred years and seeing nothing but fog and vapour he is out of spirits too; and when there is no selling or buying, or no business to settle, he prefers being alone, and looking at the fire. If any gentleman were in distress, he would willingly lend a helping hand; but he thinks it no part of neighbourhood to talk to a person because he happens to be near him. In short, with many excellent qualities, it must be acknowledged that the English are the most disagreeable of all the nations in Europe.

SYDNEY SMITH

The English are not poetical or musical or clever – they're very stupid and heavy – but they are for reasonable and constitutional liberty, that a man should have his own opinion without being knocked on the head for it.

ALFRED TENNYSON

Sir (said he), two men of any other nation who are shown into a room together, at a house where they are both visitors, will immediately find some conversation. But two Englishmen will probably go each to a different window and remain in obstinate silence.

JAMES BOSWELL, *Life of Samuel Johnson*

Mist, lumber rooms, country houses, sheep, mist, after-dinner speeches, freedom, dole: mist, Round Table, social ladder, Olympus, mist, Robinson Crusoe, autograph-albums, mist, Pegasus, castles-in-the-air.

EMILE CAMMAERTS, *Discoveries in England*

One of the greatest qualities which have made the English a great people is their eminently sane, reasonable, fairminded inability to conceive that any viewpoint save their own can possibly have the slightest merit.

STEVIE SMITH

The Oxford Voice

When you hear it languishing
and hooing and cooing and sidling through the front teeth,
     the oxford voice
       or worse still
     the would-be oxford voice
you don't even laugh any more, you can't.

For every blooming bird is an oxford cuckoo nowadays,
you can't sit on a bus nor in the tube
but it breathes gently and languishingly in the back of your
   neck.

And oh, so seductively superior, so seductively
     self-effacingly
     deprecatingly
       superior. –
We wouldn't insist on it for a moment
     but we are
      we are
    you admit we are
     superior.–

D. H. LAWRENCE

The Enquiry in England is not whether a man has talent and
   genius
But whether he is Passive and Polite and Virtuous,
As obedient to Noblemen's opinions in Art and Science.
If he is, he is a Good man. If not, he must be starved.

WILLIAM BLAKE

I know a good Christian of Hamburg who could never suppress his discontent at the fact that our Lord and Saviour was a Jew by birth. A deep fit of ill-humour seized hold of him every time when forced to confess that the Man who was a model of perfection and deserved the greatest veneration, yet belonged to the race of those pockethandkerchiefless, long-nosed Jews whom he saw hawking as pedlars about the streets, and whom he so heartily hated; and who were yet more fatal to him when they took to high commerce and dealt in spices and logwood, and so interfered with his own interests.

Shakespeare and I stood in somewhat similar relations as Jesus Christus did to this son of Hammonia (Hamburg). My spirit sinks within me when I reflect that he after all was an Englishman, and belonged to the most repulsive set of people that God in His anger ever created.

What a repulsive people! What an unexhilarating country! How starched, how commonplace, how selfish, how narrow, how English! A country which the ocean had long ago gulped down if it had not been afraid of being horribly sick at stomach. A people which is a grizzly yawning monster, which breathes nothing but poisonous vapour and deadly spleen, and which in the end will certainly hang itself with a colossal ship's cable. And in such a country, among such a people, did William Shakespeare see the light of the world in April 1564!

HEINRICH HEINE, *Shakespeare's Maids and Women*

That shop-girls, work-women, domestic servants and all females in similar positions, were expressly designed for the amusement of gentlemen, and generally serve that purpose, is a proposition assented to by a large proportion of Englishmen, even when they do not act upon the idea themselves.

CHARLES ASTOR BRISTED, *Five Years in an English University*

We are persuaded that the Englishman is sexually so repressed that by an unconscious reaction he enjoys inflicting physical pain, and much fuss is made about legal, school, and nursery floggings. Personally, I think that these are hang-overs from his penal system, which certainly was the most barbarous in

Europe, and still is in some ways. . . . As to whipping noisy and disobedient small boys, I have no compunction on that point: they deserve all they get. Then, too, we hear a lot about his tendency to homosexuality. I don't see that he is worse than Frenchmen or Roumanians or the Moslem peoples – and anyway, the Germans have put him quite in the shade. No; my real objection to him as a male is that he will not give enough time, trouble or attention to the sexual act, and thereby makes it as flat, stale and deadly as a slab of one of his own cold suet puddings. In brief: in bed, he's boring.

Thanks to those lurid modern English novelists who are most read abroad, the Englishwoman is supposed to be capable of bestial excesses – especially when she travels to the East, and succumbs to the glamorous Egyptian donkey-boy or the virile Arab sheikh. (Oh, Lord! Oh, Lord! What *tripe* the English write about the Orient!) A veritable Messalina, poor dear. When, however, the European deals with her himself, he usually discovers that, though she is quite healthily sexual, she too is repressed, so that she requires a lead. It is commonly said that she yields 'all except all', insisting that a door should be ajar, neither completely open nor completely closed – like the American, I imagine, but totally unlike the average Continental woman. Judging from what I have seen in English parks and the countryside, this must be true, for both sexes resort to a mutual and public masturbation. Since I am a Latin, the demi-vierge is anathema to me. You surrender everything normally, or you stay inviolably chaste.

But, speaking broadly, the Englishwomen, though they may not go to extremes, impress me as being definitely sex-hungry. We think that the Englishman is apt to be selfish and masterful, spoilt through and through by his women, who run after him, are subservient to him, and put up with a formidable amount of egoism on his part. It looks, to an outside observer, as though they dance attendance on him far more than he does on them. This must be because there are not enough men to go round in this country. The women know it, and it engenders in them a sort of panic: that life is going to pass them by; that they will be left on the shelf; that they will never be desired. I suppose it is the profound subconscious dread of this irreparable defeat that urges them to show a man that they can be caressed for the asking. They respond so easily to his advances; and are neither self-protective nor self-interested, in the French sense of the word. I am horrified at the way in which they allow themselves to be picked up and plumped down again with the most callous and shattering thump. . . .

I am convinced that it is this very attitude which helps to make the Englishman such an unsatisfactory lover. He is so accustomed to a quick unopposed success that he no longer takes any pains to study an 'approach'. He does not think he has to. Again and again I have been amazed at what happens to me in the parks, when I am sitting quietly in a chair with a book. An Englishman arrives, bows, and squats down on the grass by my side. (And here I must stress the fact that I am NOT a young woman. So it cannot be real attraction; it must be habit.) He talks to me about the weather – so politely that it is impossible to reply only by a grunt. After two minutes: 'Won't you come for a drive in my car?' he asks. (What a preponderant role the owner-driven car plays in the sexual relationships of the English!) Or: 'Won't you come and have tea in my flat? It's just round the corner.'

'No, I won't,' I answer, roused (even though he *is* an Englishman!). 'And why the hell you should assume that I'm starving for cheap copulation, I cannot imagine. Will you please take the trouble to find out whether I wish to be courted or not, before you make your suggestions?'

'Why, what's wrong with them?' says the Englishman, genuinely surprised. 'Oh, come, don't be so prudish! *Surely you like it!*' I've underlined his words, which are invariable, because they are so significant: I'm not asked if I like *him*, but *it*. He speaks in good faith. How can I help concluding that he is so rarely repulsed, in his desire for a casual and irresponsible flutter, by his own women, that he takes their assent as a matter of course? I do not pretend for a moment that I consider this to be 'immorality', or that I am shocked at his impulses. Most of these men, one discovers later, are free. But it is his certainty of the woman's immediate acquiescence that scandalizes me; and how deplorable it is that he should have been permitted to grow so vain, thick-skinned, and selfish! No wonder that when the Englishmen do marry, they conduct themselves towards their wives with the light touch of pachyderms.

ODETTE KEUN, *I Discover the English*

It is hard to imagine what justification the English suppose themselves to have when they sneer gently at the Spaniards for their alleged *mañana, mañana*. Probably the fact is that everyone is much lazier than he likes to admit, and, when he finds himself procrastinating wildly comforts himself with the thought that someone across the seas is lazier still. . . . If I wrote a book about England I should call it *What about Wednesday Week?*, which is what English people say when they are making what they believe to be an urgent appointment.

CLAUD COCKBURN, *In Time of Trouble*

No Englishman can live without something to complain of.

WILLIAM HAZLITT

Why is the Englishman so tongue-tied? Because he ought to be a poet, but has enough sense to know he isn't one. Englishmen never find their tongue except in public telephone booths, where the person addressed is invisible, or in after-dinner speeches, where the persons addressed are indistinguishable. But for the most part the English keep themselves to themselves, without taking much trouble to make their own company worthwhile.

HUGH KINGSMILL, *This Blessed Plot* (with Hesketh Pearson)

LONDON

❦

They rattled on through the noisy, bustling, crowded streets of London, now displaying long double rows of brightly-burning lamps, dotted here and there with the chemists' glaring lights, and illuminated besides with the brilliant flood that streamed from the windows of the shops, where sparkling jewellery, silks and velvets of the richest colours, the most inviting delicacies, and most sumptuous articles of luxurious ornament, succeeded each other in rich and glittering profusion. Streams of people apparently without end poured on and on, jostling each other in the crowd and hurrying forward, scarcely seeming to notice the riches that surrounded them on every side; while vehicles of all shapes and makes, mingled up together in one moving mass like running water, lent their ceaseless roar to swell the noise and tumult.

As they dashed by the quickly-changing and ever-varying objects, it was curious to observe in what a strange procession they passed before the eye. Emporiums of splendid dresses, the materials brought from every quarter of the world; tempting stores of every thing to stimulate and pamper the sated appetite and give new relish to the oft-repeated feast; vessels of burnished gold and silver, wrought into every exquisite form of vase, and dish, and goblet; guns, swords, pistols, and patent engines of destruction; screws and irons for the crooked, clothes for the newly-born, drugs for the sick, coffins for the dead, and churchyards for the buried – all these jumbled each with the other and flocking side by side, seemed to flit by in motley dance like the fantastic groups of the old Dutch painter, and with the same stern moral for the unheeding restless crowd.

Nor were there wanting objects in the crowd itself to give new point and purpose to the shifting scene. The rags of the squalid ballad-singer fluttered in the rich light that showed the goldsmith's treasures, pale and pinched-up faces hovered about the windows where was tempting food, hungry eyes wandered over the profusion guarded by one thin sheet of brittle glass – an iron wall to them; half-naked shivering figures stopped to gaze at Chinese shawls and golden stuffs of

India. There was a christening party at the largest coffin-maker's, and a funeral hatchment had stopped some great improvements in the bravest mansion. Life and death went hand in hand; wealth and poverty stood side by side; repletion and starvation laid them down together.

But it was London; and the old country lady inside, who had put her head out of the coach-window a mile or two this side of Kingston, and cried out to the driver that she was sure he must have passed it and forgotten to set her down, was satisfied at last.

CHARLES DICKENS, *Nicholas Nickleby*

An American gentleman observed that, when he first came to London, all the people in the streets 'seemed as if they were going on an *errand*, and had been charged to *make haste back*'. Never was there a better description.

WILLIAM COBBETT

London, that great sea, whose ebb and flow
At once is deaf and loud, and on the shore
Vomits its wrecks, and still howls on for more.

PERCY BYSSHE SHELLEY

Anyone who has ever visited London must have been at least once in the Haymarket at night. It is a district in certain streets of which prostitutes swarm by night in their thousands. Streets are lit by jets of gas – something completely unknown in our own country. At every step you come across magnificent public houses, all mirrors and gilt. They serve as meeting places as well as shelters. It is a terrifying experience to find oneself in that crowd. And, what an odd amalgam it is. You will find old women there and beautiful women at the sight of whom you stop in amazement. There are no women in the world as beautiful as the English.

The streets can hardly accommodate the dense, seething crowd. The mob has not enough room on the pavements and swamps the whole street. All this mass of humanity craves for booty and hurls itself at the first comer with shameless cynicism. Glistening, expensive clothes and semi-rags and sharp differences in age – they are all there. A drunken tramp shuffling along in this terrible crowd is jostled by the rich and titled. You hear curses, quarrels, solicitations and the quiet, whispered invitation of some still bashful beauty. And how beautiful they sometimes are with their keepsake faces! I remember once I went into a 'casino'. The music was blaring, people were dancing, a huge crowd was milling around. The place was magnificently decorated. But gloom never forsakes the English even in the midst of gaiety; even when they dance they look serious, not to say sullen, making hardly any steps and then only as if in execution of some duty. Upstairs, in the gallery I saw a girl and stopped in amazement. She was sitting at a little table together with an apparently rich and respectable young man who, by all the signs, was an unaccustomed visitor to the casino. Perhaps he had been looking for her and they had at last found each other and arranged to meet there. He spoke to her little and only in short, jerky phrases as if he was not talking about what really interested him. Their conversation was punctuated by long and frequent silences. She, too, looked sad. Her face was delicate and fine, and there was something deep-hidden and sad, something thoughtful and melancholy in the proud expression of her eyes. I should say she had consumption. Mentally and morally she was, she could not fail to be, above the whole crowd of those wretched women; otherwise, what meaning would there be in a human face? All the same, however, she was then and there drinking gin, paid for by the young man. At last he got up, shook hands with her and went away. He left the casino, while she, her pale cheeks now flushed deep with drink, was soon lost in the crowd of women trading in their bodies.

In the Haymarket I noticed mothers who brought their little daughters to make them ply that same trade. Little girls, aged about twelve, seize you by the arm and beg you to come with them. I remember once amidst the crowd of people in the street I saw a little girl, not older than six, all in rags, dirty, bare-foot and hollow-cheeked; she had been severely beaten, and her body, which showed through the rags, was covered with bruises. She was walking along, as if oblivious of everybody and everything, in no hurry to get anywhere, and Heaven knows why loafing about in that crowd; perhaps she was hungry. Nobody was paying any attention to her. But what struck me most was the look of such distress, such hopeless despair on her face that to see that tiny bit of humanity already bearing the imprint of all that evil and despair was somehow unnatural and terribly painful. She kept on shaking her tousled head as if arguing about something, gesticulated and spread her little hands and then suddenly clasped them together and pressed them to her little bare breast. I went back and gave her sixpence. She took the small silver coin, gave me a wild look of frightened surprise, and suddenly ran off as fast as her legs could carry her, as if afraid that I should take the money away from her. Jolly scenes, altogether. . . .

And then one night in the midst of a crowd of loose women and debauchees I was stopped by a woman making her way hurriedly through it. She was dressed all in black and her hat almost concealed her face; in fact I had hardly time to make it out, I only remember the steady gaze of her eyes. She said something in broken French which I failed to understand, thrust a piece of paper into my hand and hurried on. I examined the paper at the light of a café window: it was a small square slip. One side bore the words 'Crois-tu cela?' printed on it. The other, also in French: 'I am the Resurrection and the Life'. . . , etc. – the well-known text. This too, you must admit, is rather bizarre. It was explained to me afterwards that there was Catholic propaganda ferreting round everywhere, persistent and tireless. Sometimes they distribute these bits of paper in the streets, sometimes booklets containing extracts from the New Testament and the Bible. They distribute them free, thrust them into people's hands, press them on people. It is ingenious and cunning propaganda. A Catholic priest would search out and insinuate himself into a poor workman's family. He would find, for example, a sick man lying in his rags on a damp floor, surrounded by children crazy from cold and hunger, with a wife famished and often drunk. He would feed them all, provide clothes and warmth for them, give treatment to the sick man, buy medicine for him, become the friend of the family and finally convert them all to the Catholic faith. Sometimes, however, after the sick man has been restored to health, the priest is driven out with curses and kicks. He does not despair and goes off to someone else. He is chucked out again, but puts up with everything and catches someone in the end.

But an Anglican minister would never visit a poor man. The poor are not even allowed inside a church because they have not the money to pay for a seat. More often than not working-class men and women and the poor generally live together in illegitimate union, as marriages are expensive. Many husbands, by the way, beat their wives horribly and disfigure them to the point of death – mostly with the aid of pokers used to break up coal in open grates. They seem to regard them specifically as instruments for beating purposes. At least, in describing family quarrels, injuries and murders, newspapers always mention pokers. The children of the poor, while still very young, often go out into the streets, merge with the crowd and in the end fail to return to their parents.

FYODOR DOSTOYEVSKY, *Winter Notes and Summer Impressions*

It begins the moment you set foot ashore, the moment you step off the boat's gangway. The heart suddenly, yet vaguely sinks. It is no lurch of fear. Quite the contrary. It is as if the life-urge failed, and the heart dimly sank. You trail past the benevolent policeman and the inoffensive passport officials, through the

fussy and somehow foolish customs – we don't *really* think it matters if somebody smuggles in two pairs of false-silk stockings – and we get into the poky but inoffensive train, with poky but utterly inoffensive people, and we have a cup of inoffensive tea from a nice inoffensive boy, and we run through small, poky but nice inoffensive country, till we are landed in the big but unexciting station of Victoria, when an inoffensive porter puts us into an inoffensive taxi and we are driven through the crowded yet strangely dull streets of London to the cosy yet strangely poky and dull place where we are going to stay. And the first half-hour in London, after some years abroad, is really a plunge of misery. The strange, the grey and uncanny, almost deathly sense of *dullness* is overwhelming. Of course, you get over it after a while, and admit that you exaggerated. You get into the rhythm of London again, and you tell yourself that it is *not* dull. And yet you are haunted all the time, sleeping or waking, with the uncanny feeling: It is dull! It is all dull! The life here is one vast complex of dullness! I am dull! I am being dulled! My spirit is being dulled! My life is dulling down to London dullness.

D. H. LAWRENCE, *Assorted Articles*

Avoiding crowds and highways, I went along Battersea Bridge, and thence by a wondrous path across cow fields, mud ditches, river embankments, over a waste expanse of what attempted to pass for country, wondrous enough in the darkening dusk, especially as I had never been there before, and the very road was uncertain. I had left my watch and my purse. I had a good stick in my hand. Boat people sate drinking about the Red House; steamers snorting about the river, each with a lantern at its nose. Old women sate in strange cottages trimming their evening fire. Bewildered-looking mysterious coke furnaces (with a very bad smell) glowed at one place, I know not why. Windmills stood silent. Blackguards, improper females, and miscellanies sauntered, harmless all. Chelsea lights burnt many-hued, bright over the water in the distance – under the great sky of silver, under the great still twilight. So I wandered full of thoughts, or of things I could not think.

THOMAS CARLYLE, letter to John Carlyle, 23 August 1840

London – the city where they purvey the most inaccurate news and produce the worst possible arguments based on information which is entirely false.

Voltaire's England

Is this London? Is this the year 1872? That peep of blue up yonder resembles the sky, and these figures that pass seem men and women. What evil dream, then, what malignant influence is upon me? Weary of surveying the poetry of the past, and listening to the amatory wails of generations, I walk down the streets, and lo! again harlots stare from the shop-windows, and the great Alhambra posters cover the dead-walls. I go to the theatre which is crowded nightly, and I listen in absolute amaze to the bestialities of *Geneviève de Brabant*. I walk in the broad day, and a dozen hands offer me indecent prints. I step into a bookseller's shop, and behold! I am recommended to purchase a reprint of the plays and novels of Mrs Aphra Behn. I buy a cheap republican newspaper, thinking that there, at least, I shall find some relief, if only in the wildest stump oratory, and I am saluted instead in these words:

> Fanny Hill. Genuine edition, illustrated. Two volumes, 2s. 6d. each. Lover's Festival, plates, 3s. 6d. Adventures of a Lady's Maid. 2s. 6d. Intrigues of a Ballet Girl. 2s. 6d. Aristotle, illustrated. 2s. French transparent cards, 1s. the set. The Bachelor's Scarf pin, containing secret photos of pretty women. 24 stamps. . . .

Stop where I may, the snake Sensualism spits its venom upon me. . . . Photographs of nude, indecent, and hideous harlots, in every possible attitude that vice can devise, flaunt from the shop-windows, gloated over by the fatuous glint of the libertine and the greedy open-mouthed stare of the day-labourer. Never was this Snake, which not all the naturalists of the world have been able to scotch, so vital and poisonous as now. It has penetrated into the very sweetshops; and there, among the commoner sorts of confectionery, may be seen this year models of the female Leg, the whole definite and elegant article as far as the thigh, with a fringe of paper cut in imitation of the female drawers and embroidered in the female fashion!

ROBERT BUCHANAN, *The Fleshly School of Poetry*

I have seen the greatest wonder which the world can show to the astonished spirit; I have seen it, and am still astonished; and still there remains fixed in my memory the stone forest of houses, and amid them the rushing stream of faces of living men with all their motley passions, all their terrible impulses of love, of hunger, and of hatred – I mean London. . . .

The stranger who wanders through the great streets of this city, and does not light upon the especial quarters of the people, sees on that account nothing, or very little, of the abundant misery which prevails in London. Only here and there at the entrance of a dark little street a ragged woman sits silently with a baby at her withered bosom, and begs with her eyes. Perhaps, if these eyes are yet beautiful, one looks into them, and is astonished at the world of sorrow which is seen therein. The ordinary beggars are old people, mostly negroes, who stand at the street corners and sweep a path for the foot passengers – a service which is very useful in muddy London – and get for it a copper coin. Poverty creeps abroad first in the evening, in company with vice and crime, out of its lurking places. It avoids the light of day so much the more anxiously, the more dreadfully that its misery contrasts with the arrogance of wealth which everywhere shows itself – hunger alone drives it forth sometimes at mid-day out of its dark alleys; and then they stand with dumb, eloquent eyes, and stare beseechingly at the rich merchant, who hurries by jingling his gold, or at the idle lord, who, like a satiated god, rides by on his lofty steed and casts from time to time an indifferent superior look on the crowd of humanity, as though they were insignificant ants, or only a mass of lower creatures whose pleasure and pain have nothing in common with his feelings. Far above the mob of humanity – who cling fast to the soil – the nobility of England float like creatures of a higher race, who regard little England only as their house of accommodation, Italy as their summer garden, Paris as their ball-room – yea, the whole world as their property. Without care and without hindrance, do they float backwards and forwards, and their gold is a talisman which charms fulfilment to wait on their maddest wishes.

HEINRICH HEINE, *English Fragments*

There is no town in the world which is more adapted for training one away from people and training one into solitude than London. The manner of life, the distances, the climate, the very multitude of the population in which personality vanishes, all this together with the absence of Continental diversions conduces to the same effect. One who knows how to live alone has nothing to fear from the tedium of London. The life here, like the air here, is bad for the weak, for the frail, for one who seeks a prop outside himself, for one who seeks welcome, sympathy, attention; the moral lungs here must be as strong as the physical lungs, whose task it is to separate oxygen from the smoky fog. The masses are saved by battling for their daily bread, the commercial classes by their absorption in heaping up wealth, and all by the bustle of business; but nervous and romantic temperaments – fond of living among people, fond of intellectual sloth and of idly luxuriating in emotion – are bored to death and fall into despair.

Wandering lonely about London, through its stony lanes and stifling passages, sometimes not seeing a step before me for the thick, opaline fog, and colliding with shadows running – I lived through a great deal.

In the evening, when my son had gone to bed, I usually went out for a walk; I scarcely ever went to see anyone; I read the newspapers and stared in taverns at the alien race, and lingered on the bridges across the Thames.

On one side the stalactites of the Houses of Parliament would loom through the darkness, ready to vanish again; on the other, the inverted bowl of St Paul's . . . and street-lamps . . . street-lamps . . . street-lamps without end in both directions. One city, full-fed, went to sleep: the other, hungry, was not yet awake – the streets were empty and nothing could be heard but the measured tread of the policeman with his lantern. I used to sit and look, and my soul would grow quieter and more peaceful. And so for all this I came to love this fearful ant-heap, where every night a hundred thousand men know not where they will lay their heads, and the police often find women and children dead of hunger beside hotels where one cannot dine for less than two pounds.

ALEXANDER HERZEN, *My Past and Thoughts*

Westminster Abbey

I do not think that it is an exaggeration to say that at the beginning of the sixteenth century it was the most beautiful of Gothic buildings. Everything which has been either taken away from it or added to it since then has done more or less to destroy this beauty, until today the exterior no longer exists as a work of art, and even in the matchless interior we are forced, if we are to receive any impression of beauty from it, to abstract our thoughts from a mass of monuments which, even apart from their incongruity with the delicate loveliness of the ancient architecture, are for the most part the most hideous specimens of false art that can be found in the whole world; mere Cockney nightmares and aberrations of the human intellect.

WILLIAM MORRIS, letter to the *Daily News*, 30 January 1889

One thing struck me in viewing this church as very remarkable. The monuments which are within reach of a walking stick are all more or less injured, by that barbarous habit which Englishmen have of seeing by the sense of touch if I may so express myself. They can never look at everything without having it in hand, nor show it to another person without touching it, with a stick if it is within reach: I have even noticed in several collections of pictures exposed for sale, a large printed inscription requesting the connoisseurs not to touch them. Besides this odd habit, which is universal, there is prevalent among these people a sort of mischievous manual wit, by which milestones are commonly defaced, directory-posts broken, and the parapets of bridges thrown into the river. Their dislike to a passage in a book is often shown by tearing the leaf, or scrawling over the page which differs from them in political opinion.

ROBERT SOUTHEY, *Letters from England*

Friday evening. The immoveableness of all things through which so many men were moving – a harsh contrast with the universal motion, the harmonious system of motions in the country, and everywhere in Nature in the dim light London appeared to be a huge place of sepulchres through which hosts of spirits were gliding.

Soon after this I saw starlings in vast flights, borne along like smoke, mist – like a body unendowed with voluntary power – now it shaped itself into a circular area inclined – now they formed a square – now a globe – now from a complete orb into an ellipse – then oblongated into a balloon with the car suspended, now a concave semicircle, still expanding or contracting, thinning or condensing, now glimmering and shivering, now thickening, deepening, blackening.

SAMUEL TAYLOR COLERIDGE, *Notebooks*

In literal and fatal instance of fact – think what ruin it is for men of any sensitive faculty to live in such a city as London is now! Take the highest and lowest state of it; you have, typically, Grosvenor Square – an aggregation of bricks and railings, with not so much architectural faculty expressed in the whole cumber of them as there is in a wasp's nest or a worm-hole; and you have the rows of houses which you look down into on the south side of the south-western line, between Vauxhall and Clapham Junction. Between those two ideals the London artist must seek his own; and in the humanity, or the vermin, of them, worship the aristocratic and scientific gods of living Israel.

JOHN RUSKIN, *The Art of England*

In every thing where *horses* are the chief instruments (and horses are second only to men) the English so far surpass all the rest of the world that there is no room for comparison. The man who has a mind to know something of England in this respect, should walk from the Tower of London to Charing Cross a little after day-light in the morning, while the streets are clear of people. He would often then see the teams of immense horses, drawing up from the bank of the Thames, coals, timber, stone and other heavy materials. One morning last summer I counted, in various places, more than a hundred of these teams worth *each of them*, harness, waggon, load and all, little less than a thousand pounds. The horses, upon an average, weigh more than a ton. But the finest sight in England is a stage coach just ready to start. A great sheep or cattle fair is a beautiful sight: but in the stage coach you see more of what man is capable of performing. The vehicle itself, the harness, all so complete and so neatly arranged; so strong and clean and good. The beautiful horses impatient to be off. The inside full and the outside covered, in every part, with men, women, children, boxes, bags, bundles. The coachman, taking his reins in one hand and his whip in the other, gives a signal with his foot, and away go, at the rate of seven miles an hour, the population and the property of a hamlet. One of these coaches coming in, after a long journey, is a sight not less interesting. The horses are now all sweat

and foam, the reek from their bodies ascending like a cloud. The whole equipage is covered perhaps with dust and dirt. But still, on it comes as steady as the hands of a clock.

As a proof of the perfection to which this mode of travelling has been brought, there is one coach which goes between Exeter and London, the proprietors of which agree to forfeit *eight pence* for every *minute* that the coach is behind its time at any of its stages; and this coach, I believe, travels eight miles an hour, and that too upon a very hilly and, at some seasons, very deep road.

WILLIAM COBBETT, *Political Register*

Speakers' Corner

The first speaker arrives: Robert Mathews of the Coloured Workers Welfare Association. He buys a cup of tea, and then wanders back across the tarmac to fetch his platform, with his cracked bowler hat on one side of his head and his briefcase, tied onto his waistband, hanging round his knees.

The West Indian known as Jahweh arrives in his white coat, dabbling with the calico strings of his wooden harp. He stands by the gate, opens his hebrew bible and begins to chant from it. His mouth begins to lather, his ringleted hair shakes in the wind. He gathers a crowd.

Van Dyn comes in the East Gate dragging his tea chest. He sits down on it, sorts out his newspaper cuttings, and wanders across to the catering stall to buy a cup of tea with no milk and five lumps of sugar. He looks about for the police and tries to sell some handbills with his photograph on them. They advertise a selection of tattoo artists, none of whom ever tattooed Van Dyn. He walks back to the tea chest, stomping the discarded paper cups with his heels. He screeches, kicks an oil drum across the tarmac and starts his meeting.

The man with the silent message hooks a milk crate from under the refreshment stall with his umbrella, brings it into the open, mounts it and reads his newspaper.

Mathews returns, drinks his tea with both hands for he has no fingers, erects his platform, climbs up on it and knocks the board at the top of it with his stumps shouting: OPPOSITION! COME ON . . . OPPOSITION! COME ON POOR WHITE BASTARD, POOR WHITE TRASH, COME ON . . . OPPOSITION . . . He gathers a crowd.

The park fills.

Platforms, notices and banners slowly rise above the heads of the listeners: THE END IS NIGH in slab letters on flapping sail cloth; THE COMMUNIST PARTY OF GREAT BRITAIN; THE PROTESTANT TRUTH SOCIETY; THE SALVATION ARMY; THE MOVEMENT FOR FREEDOM IN KASHMIR; THE CATHOLIC EVIDENCE GUILD; THE MOVEMENT OF PAN-AFRICAN EXPONENTS AND OF PEOPLES OF AFRICAN DESCENT, and beneath it: GIVE US THE LIBERTY TO KNOW, UTTER AND TO ARGUE FREELY ACCORDING TO CONSCIENCE ABOVE ALL LIBERTY; THE NATIONAL SECULAR SOCIETY; THE EX-SERVICE MOVEMENT FOR PEACE; THE NATURAL LAW RELIGION; POBLACHT OIBRITHE IN EIREAN AR GCUSPOIR: THE CAUSE OF LABOUR IS THE CAUSE OF IRELAND, written awkwardly on a board, the outside layer of wood corrugated with the rain; THE SOCIETY FOR EVANGELIZING LONDON; HOW THE WAR OFFICE ROBS INVENTORS; Stanley Broder's INDIVIDUALISM; and then the faint syllogism of the Church Army: GOD loves you. GOD wants you. YOU need God.

HEATHCOTE WILLIAMS, The Speakers

A Spellbound Palace (Hampton Court)

On this kindly yellow day of mild low-travelling winter sun
      The stirless depths of the yews
      Are vague with misty blues:
Across the spacious pathways stretching spires of shadow run,
And the wind-gnawed walls of ancient brick are fired vermil-
      ion.

    Two or three early sanguine finches tune
  Some tentative strains, to be enlarged by May or June:
      From a thrush or blackbird
      Comes now and then a word,
While an enfeebled fountain somewhere within is heard.

      Our footsteps wait awhile.
      Then draw beneath the pile,
      When an inner court outspreads
      As 'twere History's own asile,
Where the now-visioned fountain its attenuate crystal sheds
In passive lapse that seems to ignore the yon world's clamorous
      clutch,
And lays an insistent numbness on the place, like a cold hand's
      touch.

And there swaggers the Shade of a straddling King, plumed,
      sworded, with sensual face,
And lo, too, that of his Minister, at a bold self-centred pace:
Sheer in the sun they pass; and thereupon all is still,
Save the mindless fountain tinkling on with thin enfeebled
      will.

THOMAS HARDY

I am pent up in frowzy lodgings, where there is not room
enough to swing a cat; and I breathe the steams of endless
putrefaction; and these would, undoubtedly, produce a pesti-
lence, if they were not qualified by the gross acid of sea-coal,
which is itself a pernicious nuisance to lungs of any delicacy of
texture: but even this boasted corrector cannot prevent those
languid, sallow looks, that distinguish the inhabitants of Lon-

don from those ruddy swains that lead a country life. I go to bed after midnight, jaded and restless from the dissipations of the day. I start every hour from my sleep, at the horrid noise of the watchmen bawling the hour through every street, and thundering at every door; a set of useless fellows, who serve no other purpose but that of disturbing the repose of the inhabitants; and by five o'clock I start out of bed, in consequence of the still more dreadful alarm made by the country carts, and noisy rustics bellowing green pease under my window. If I would drink water, I must quaff the maukish contents of an open aqueduct, exposed to all manner of defilement; or swallow that which comes from the river Thames, impregnated with all the filth of London and Westminster. Human excrement is the least offensive part of the concrete, which is composed of all the drugs, minerals, and poisons, used in mechanics and manufacture, enriched with the putrefying carcases of beasts and men; and mixed with the scourings of all the wash-tubs, kennels, and common sewers, within the bills of mortality. . . .

A companionable man will, undoubtedly, put up with many inconveniencies for the sake of enjoying agreeable society. A facetious friend of mine used to say, the wine could not be bad, where the company was agreeable; a maxim which, however, ought to be taken *cum grano salis*; but what is the society of London, that I should be tempted, for its sake, to mortify my senses, and compound with such uncleanness as my soul abhors? All the people I see, are too much engrossed by schemes of interest or ambition, to have any room left for sentiment or friendship. Even in some of my old acquaintance, those schemes and pursuits have obliterated all traces of our former connexion. Conversation is reduced to party disputes, and illiberal altercation; social commerce, to formal visits and card-playing. If you pick up a diverting original by accident, it may be dangerous to amuse yourself with his oddities: he is generally a tartar at bottom; a sharper, a spy, or a lunatic. Every person you deal with endeavours to over-reach you in the way of business; you are preyed upon by idle mendicants, who beg in the phrase of borrowing, and live upon the spoils of the stranger. Your tradesmen are without conscience, your friends without affection, and your dependants without fidelity.

TOBIAS SMOLLETT, *Humphrey Clinker*

It would be a folly in me to attempt giving you any kind of a description of London, which seems to me like a world of itself, containing all kinds of characters, from the very best, to the very worst of the human race – all seemed busily intent in pursuit of their several callings, and put me in mind of an immense ant-hill putting all to rights again, after being disturbed by being stirred up, and turned over with a stick from top to bottom, which I used to do when a boy, before I had begun to reflect upon the misery I had thus occasioned – the real Cockneys seem to me to be no way altered in character – since I left them above fifty-one years ago – they are still fond of high living and talk in the same way about 'good wittals' – one of them, while I waited for the Barber to shave me, could not wait his return, but set to work to scrape off his own black beard himself – singing all the while to a tune which he thought was music and taking care to make it known that he had eaten a 'full pound' of beef steaks before getting his tea – it struck me again, that these little, fat lumps of the human species were in the caterpillar state and would always remain so.

THOMAS BEWICK, letter to John Dovaston, 10 September 1828

I was hurrying along Cheapside into Newgate Street among a thousand bustling pigmies and the innumerable jinglings and rollings and crashings of many-coloured Labour when all at once I looked up from the boiling through a little opening at the corner of the street – and there stood St Paul's – with its columns and friezes, and massy wings of bleached yet unworn stone; with its statues and its graves around it; with its solemn dome four hundred feet above me, and its gilded ball and cross gleaming in the evening sun, piercing up into heaven through the vapours of our earthly home! It was as silent as Tadmor of the Wilderness; gigantic, beautiful, enduring; it seemed to frown with a rebuking pity on the vain scramble which it overlooked: at its feet were tombstones, above it was the everlasting sky, within priests perhaps were chanting hymns; it seemed to transmit with a stern voice the sounds of Death, Judgment, and Eternity through all the frivolous and fluctuating city.

THOMAS CARLYLE, letter to Alexander Carlyle, 25 June 1824

I wander thro' each charter'd street,
Near where the charter'd Thames does flow,
And mark in every face I meet
Marks of weakness, marks of woe.

In every cry of every man,
In every infant's cry of fear,
In every voice, in every ban,
The mind-forg'd manacles I hear.

How the chimney-sweeper's cry
Every black'ning church appals;
And the hapless soldier's sigh
Runs in blood down palace walls.

But most thro' midnight streets I hear
How the youthful harlot's curse
Blasts the new-born infant's tear,
And blights with plagues the marriage hearse.

WILLIAM BLAKE

There is still something that recalls to me the enchantments of children – the anticipation of Christmas, the delight of a holiday walk – in the way the shop-fronts shine into the fog. It makes each of them seem a little world of light and warmth, and I can still waste time in looking at them with dirty Bloomsbury on one side and dirtier Soho on the other. There are winter effects, not intrinsically sweet, it would appear, which somehow, in absence, touch the chords of memory and even the fount of tears: as for instance the front of the British Museum on a black afternoon, or the portico, when the weather is vile, of one of the big square clubs in Pall Mall. I can give no adequate account of the subtle poetry of such reminiscences; it depends upon associations of which we have often lost the thread. The wide colonnade of the Museum, its symmetrical wings, the high iron fence in its granite setting, the sense of the misty halls within, where all the treasures lie –

these things loom patiently through atmospheric layers which instead of making them dreary impart to them something of a cheer of red lights in a storm. I think the romance of a winter afternoon in London arises partly from the fact that, when it is not altogether smothered, the general lamplight takes this hue of hospitality. Such is the colour of the interior glow of the clubs in Pall Mall, which I positively like best when the fog loiters upon their monumental staircases.

HENRY JAMES, *Essays in London*

London never had any formal or obvious beauty, such as you find in Paris; or any great, overwhelming grandeur, such as Rome has. But the districts for which I loved her, and several other districts too, had a queer beauty of their own, and were intensely characteristic – inalienably Londonish. To an intelligent foreigner, visiting London for the first time, what would you hasten to show? Except some remnants here and there, and some devious little nooks, there is nothing that would excite or impress him. The general effect of the buildings that have sprung up everywhere in recent years is not such an effect as the intelligent foreigner may not have seen in divers other places – Chicago, for example, or Berlin, or Pittsburg. London has been cosmopolitanized, democratized, commercialized, mechanized, standardized, vulgarized, so extensively that one's pride in showing it to a foreigner is changed to a wholesome humility. One feels rather as Virgil may have felt in showing Hell to Dante.

MAX BEERBOHM, *Mainly on the Air*

Eros and Psyche

In an old dull yard near Camden Town,
Which echoes with the rattle of cars and 'buses
And freight-trains, puffing steam and smoke and dirt
To the steaming sooty sky –
There stands an old and grimy statue,
A statue of Psyche and her lover, Eros.

A little nearer Camden Town,
In a square of ugly sordid shops,
Is another statue, facing the Tube,
Staring with heavy purposeless glare
At the red and white shining tiles –
A tall stone statue of Cobden.
And though no one ever pauses to see
What hero it is that faces the Tube,
I can understand very well indeed
That England must honour its national heroes,
Must honour the hero of Free Trade –
Or was it the Corn Laws? –
That I can understand.

But what I shall never understand
Is the little group in the dingy yard
Under the dingier sky,
The Eros and Psyche –
Surrounded with pots and terra-cotta busts
And urns and broken pillars –
Eros, naked, with his wings stretched out
Just lighting down to kiss her on the lips.

What are they doing here in Camden Town
In the midst of all this clamour and filth?
They, who should stand in a sun-lit room
Hung with deep purple, painted with gods,
Paved with dark porphyry,
Stand for ever embraced
By the side of a rustling fountain
Over a marble basin
Carved with leopards and grapes and young men dancing;
Or in a garden leaning above Corinth,
Under the ilexes and the cypresses,
Very white against a very blue sky;
Or growing hoary, if they must grow old,
With lichens and softly creeping moss:
What are they doing here in Camden Town?
And who has brought their naked beauty
And their young fresh lust to Camden Town,
Which settled long ago to toil and sweat and filth,

Forgetting – to the greater glory of Free Trade –
Young beauty and young love and youthful flesh?

Slowly the rain settles down on them,
Slowly the soot eats into them,
Slowly the stone grows greyer and dirtier,
Till in spite of his spreading wings
Her eyes have a rim of soot
Half an inch deep,
And his wings, the tall god's wings,
That should be red and silver
Are ocherous brown.

And I peer from a 'bus-top
As we splash through the grease and puddles,
And I glimpse them, huddled against the wall,
Half-hidden under a freight-train's smoke,
And I see the limbs that a Greek slave cut
In some old Italian town,
I see them growing older
And sadder
And greyer.

RICHARD ALDINGTON

London Lunch Hours (from the diaries of Barbara Pym)

1961. A rather rich lunch hour in St Paul's churchyard. All the people sitting on seats with lunch, knitting etc., raising their faces to the mild September sun. I go round to the back where the pieces of broken marble are – it is all white and beautiful, looks good enough to eat – broken off bits of friezes and urn stands. In the middle of such a pile, as if on the rocks at the seaside, sits a woman (middle-aged of course) drinking tea from a plastic cup, the traffic swirling in front of her. I pass the mulberry tree, but it is too late for there to be squashed mulberries on the pavement. Coming round the other side and down by the shops I go to the second-hand bookshop. There is a band playing on the steps of St Paul's which can be heard in the shop. It is a boys' band and they play the Pilgrims' Chorus from

Tannhäuser at which point inconsequential conversation starts in the shop between the owner and a woman about dogs/cats . . .

4 February 1972. Lunch in the Kingsway Kardomah reading the *Church Times* (even that has gone off – no Answers to Correspondents). A tiny little elderly woman clears the tables – only about 5 ft high or less so that one nearly knocks her over with one's tray. Her little wrinkled claw-like hand comes towards

me with a J-cloth to wipe the counter. Go away, old crone, I want to say. The best place to sit is in the window, watching the cars come down Kingsway and stopping at the zebra crossings. The *only* places to have lunch now: Kingsway Kardomah, Holborn Kardomah (The Dutch House), Gay Fayre opposite the Prudential – very squashed but one could sit in the window there on a high stool and watch Gamages being demolished. Then the Tea Centre in Lower Regent St is good too. 'You get a nice class of person there.'

20 March 1972. The ABC café in Fleet St, opposite the Law Courts – new but ever old. The new name (The Light Bite), the smart orange and olive green and beige and stripped pine decor, the hanging lamp shades, the new green crockery – but inside the food is the same, the little woman cooking, the West

Indian lady serving the tea, the nice, bright efficient lady at the cash desk.

10 May 1972. Sitting at lunch in the help-yourself in Bourne and Hollingsworth I think why, those women sitting round me are like lunatics in some colour supplement photographs of bad conditions in a mental home. Twitching or slumping or bending low over their food like an animal at a dish (especially if eating *spaghetti*).

A Very Private Eye

Dear, old-fashioned, leisurely, traditional, eccentric London is a legend we have successfully sold to foreigners, even to ourselves. London fails to look splendid because it is a hard place, hard as nails.

V. S. PRITCHETT, *London Perceived*

Business Girls

From the geyser ventilators
  Autumn winds are blowing down
On a thousand business women
  Having baths in Camden Town.

Waste pipes chuckle into runnels,
  Steam's escaping here and there,
Morning trains through Camden cutting
  Shake the crescent and the Square.

Early nip of changeful autumn,
  Dahlias glimpsed through garden doors,
At the back precarious bathrooms
  Jutting out from upper floors;

And behind their frail partitions
  Business women lie and soak,
Seeing through the draughty skylight
  Flying clouds and railway smoke.

Rest you there, poor unbelov'd ones,
   Lap your loneliness in heat.
All too soon the tiny breakfast,
   Trolley-bus and windy street!

JOHN BETJEMAN

I once met a man walking up Charing Cross Road accompanied by a small elephant. There was a certain element of incongruity in this spectacle, one might even call it surprising. But what surprised me more than the elephant and its companion was the minimum of attention which they attracted. To say that no one took any notice of them would be an understatement. A good many passers-by turned round and stared, while some stopped and gazed after the pair. But they created little comment and no stir.

The most delightful thing about London is that nobody minds what anyone does or says – within the bounds of morality. There is an individual freedom about the place which fittingly symbolizes the English spirit. Barrie is held to have said that the chief thing about London is that you can eat a bun in the street without drawing attention to yourself. You need not wear a hat. No garb is laughed at: a man clothed in the flowing robes of a Franciscan Friar with long hair down his neck will occasion as little surprise as a parrot perched on someone's shoulder – while during a heat-wave there is such an extremity of unconventionality as to scandalize foreigners who do not understand the effect which a few days' continuous sunshine has upon English people. Anyone may talk to himself aloud without notice: indeed, the number of persons who smile and chat to themselves alone as they walk through the streets makes up for their reserve when they get together.

JOHN STEWART COLLIS, *An Irishman's England*

A London Suburb

There is much going on in the suburb for those who seek company. There is the Shakespeare Reading Society, the Allotment

Growers' Club; there is a Players' Society in connection with the local theatre; there are the amateur dramatic societies (that are such a delicious hotbed of the emotions – chagrin, display, the managerial mind; pleasure in becoming for one evening a spiv or a lord; ingenuity, competition, meeting young men). There are also the games clubs and the political clubs – tennis, golf, cycling; conservative, labour, communist. There is skating on the indoor rinks, and when the frost is hard, skating too on the great lake in Scapelands Park. There is also riding on the spavined hack or, for those who like danger, on the 'chaser whose temper is as vile as his price was low. The anglers who fish the inshore waters of Scapelands Lake have also their club, but theirs is a silent fellowship. Even the young boys fish silently, but sometimes a bite will stir them to words – 'Hang on, man.'

The most beautiful place in the suburb is Scapelands Park, especially when the weather is wild and there is nobody about except the anglers. When the wind blows east and ruffles the water of the lake, driving the rain before it, the Egyptian geese rise with a squawk, and the rhododendron trees, shaken by the gusts, drip the raindrops from the blades of their green-black leaves. The empty park, in the winter rain, has a staunch and inviolate melancholy that is refreshing. For are not sometimes the brightness and busyness of suburbs, the common life and the chatter, the kiddy-cars on the pavements and the dogs, intolerable?

Christianity in the suburb is cheerful. The church is a centre of social activity and those who go to church need never be lonely. The stained glass windows in the church, which are of the Burne-Jones' school and not very good, have been sub-scribed for by loving relations to commemorate the friends of the church and the young men killed in the wars. There is cheerfulness and courage in the church community, and mod-esty in doing good. . . .

In Scapelands Park of a fine Sunday afternoon you may snuff the quick-witted high-flying life of a true suburban community. Here the young girls swing arm in arm round the path that borders the still lake-water. As they swing past the boys who are coming to meet them, the girls cry out, to the boys, 'Okey-doke, phone me.' In the deck chair beside the pavilion the old gentleman is talking to his friend, 'It is my birthday today and my wife would have me adorned. She put this suit on me' (he points to the flower in his buttonhole) 'and sent to have me adorned.' By the cage of budgerigars sits the ageing Miss Cattermole, who is rather mad. She wears a pink scarf 'to keep the evil spirits away'. She says the vicar is plotting to kill her. . . .

'Mother,' says the child, 'is that a dog of good family?' She is pointing to a puppy bulldog of seven weeks old; his face is softly wrinkled. His tight velvet skin has already the delicate markings of the full-grown brindle dog. His stomach is fat as the new-born.

Dogs in suburbs are very popular and are not trained at all not to bark. 'Why should my dog not bark if he wants to?' is rather the idea. It is a free country, they also say. But not apparently so free that you do not have to listen to the dogs barking.

Once, waking early, I heard the dog-loving woman from the next house but one talking to her friend in the street below my window. This is what she was saying:

> 'Seven years old 'e is.
> Ever so sweet 'e is.
> Ever such a neat coat 'e's got.
> Ever so fond of kiddies.
> But a dog likes to know oo's going to 'it 'im
>   and oo isn't.'

This is the unconscious poem that happens sometimes when people are talking.

It would be wrong to suppose that everything always goes well in the suburbs. At Number 71, the wife does not speak to her husband, he is a gentle creature, retired now for many years from the Merchant Navy. He paces the upstairs rooms. His wife sits downstairs; she is a vegetarian and believes in earth currents; she keeps a middle-aged daughter in subjection. At Number 5, the children were taught to steal the milk from the doorsteps. They were clever at this, the hungry dirty children. Their father was a mild man, but the mother loved the violent lodger. When they were sent to prison for neglecting the children, the lodger bailed the mother out but let the father lie.

Life in the suburbs is richer at the lower levels. At these levels the people are not selfconscious at all, they are at liberty to be as eccentric as they please, they do not know that they are eccentric. At the more expensive levels the people have bridge parties and say of their neighbours, 'They are rather suburban.'

The virtue of the suburb lies in this: it is wide open to the sky, it is linked to the city, it is linked to the country, the air blows fresh, it is a cheap place for families to live in and have children and gardens: it smells of lime trees, tar, cut grass, roses, it has clear colours that are not smudged by London soot, as are the heath at Hampstead and the graceful slopes of Primrose Hill. In the streets and gardens are the pretty trees – laburnum, monkey puzzle, mountain ash, the rose, the rhododendron, the lilac. And behind the fishnet curtains in the windows of the houses is the family life – father's chair, uproar, dogs, babies and radio.

STEVIE SMITH, *Me Again*

Midnight in London

The heavy bell of St Paul's tolled for the death of another day. Midnight had come upon the crowded city. The palace, the night-cellar, the jail, the madhouse, the chambers of birth and death, of health and sickness, the rigid face of the corpse and the calm sleep of the child: midnight was upon them all.

CHARLES DICKENS, *Oliver Twist*

HOME SWEET HOME

◆§ §◆

After my work in the City, I like to be at home! What's the good of a home, if you are never in it? 'Home Sweet Home'; that's my motto.

GEORGE AND WEEDON GROSSMITH, Diary of a Nobody

Dulce Domum

The rapid nightfall of mid-December had quite beset the little village as they approached it on soft feet over a first thin fall of powdery snow. Little was visible but squares of a dusky orange-red on either side of the street, where the firelight or lamplight of each cottage overflowed through the casements into the dark world without. Most of the low latticed windows were innocent of blinds, and to the lookers-in from outside, the inmates, gathered round the tea-table, absorbed in handiwork, or talking with laughter and gesture, had each that happy grace which is the last thing the skilled actor shall capture – the natural grace which goes with perfect unconsciousness of observation. Moving at will from one theatre to another, the two spectators, so far from home themselves, had something of wistfulness in their eyes as they watched a cat being stroked, a sleepy child picked up and huddled off to bed, or a tired man stretch and knock out his pipe on the end of a smouldering log.

But it was from one little window, with its blind drawn down, a mere blank transparency on the night, that the sense of home and the little curtained world within walls – the larger stressful world of outside Nature shut out and forgotten – most pulsated. Close against the white blind hung a bird-cage, clearly silhouetted, every wire, perch, and appurtenance distinct and recognizable, even to yesterday's dull-edged lump of sugar. On the middle perch the fluffy occupant, head tucked well into feathers, seemed so near to them as to be easily stroked, had they tried; even the delicate tips of his plumped-out plumage pencilled plainly on the illuminated screen. As they looked, the sleepy little fellow stirred uneasily, woke, shook himself, and raised his head. They could see the gape of his tiny beak as he yawned in a bored sort of way, looked round, and then settled his head into his back again, while the ruffled feathers gradually subsided into perfect stillness. Then a gust of bitter wind took them in the back of the neck, a small sting of frozen sleet on the skin woke them as from a dream, and they knew their toes to be cold and their legs tired, and their own home distant a weary way.

Once beyond the village, where the cottages ceased abruptly, on either side of the road they could smell through the darkness the friendly fields again; and they braced themselves for the last long stretch, the home stretch, the stretch that we know is bound to end, some time, in the rattle of the door-latch, the sudden firelight, and the sight of familiar things greeting us as long-absent travellers from far oversea. They plodded along steadily and silently, each of them thinking his own thoughts. The Mole's ran a good deal on supper, as it was pitch dark, and it was all a strange country to him as far as he knew, and he was following obediently in the wake of the Rat, leaving the guidance entirely to him. As for the Rat, he was walking a little way ahead, as his habit was, his shoulders humped, his eyes fixed on the straight grey road in front of him; so he did not notice poor Mole when suddenly the summons reached him, and took him like an electric shock.

We others, who have long lost the more subtle of the physical senses, have not even proper terms to express an animal's intercommunications with his surroundings, living or otherwise, and have only the word 'smell', for instance, to include the whole range of delicate thrills which murmur in the nose of the animal night and day, summoning, warning, inciting, repelling. It was one of these mysterious fairy calls from out the void that suddenly reached Mole in the darkness, making him tingle through and through with its very familiar appeal, even while as yet he could not clearly remember what it was. He stopped dead in his tracks, his nose searching hither and thither in its efforts to recapture the fine filament, the telegraphic current, that had so strongly moved him. A moment, and he had caught it again; and with it this time came recollection in fullest flood.

Home! That was what they meant, those caressing appeals, those soft touches wafted through the air, those invisible little hands pulling and tugging, all one way! Why, it must be quite close by him at that moment, his old home that he had hurriedly forsaken and never sought again, that day when he first found the river! And now it was sending out its scouts and its messengers to capture him and bring him in. Since his escape on that bright morning he had hardly given it a thought, so absorbed had he been in his new life, in all its pleasures, its surprises, its fresh and captivating experiences. Now, with a rush of old memories, how clearly it stood up before him, in the darkness! Shabby indeed, and small and poorly furnished, and yet his, the home he had made for himself, the home he had been so happy to get back to after his day's work. And the home had been happy with him, too, evidently, and was missing him, and wanted him back, and was telling him so, through his nose, sorrowfully, reproachfully, but with no bitterness or anger; only with plaintive reminder that it was there, and wanted him.

KENNETH GRAHAME, *The Wind in the Willows*

If on any night at the busiest part of the theatrical season in London the audiences were cordoned by the police and examined individually as to their views on the subject, there would probably not be a single house-owning native among them who would not conceive a visit to the theatre, or indeed to any public assembly, artistic or political, as an exceptional way of spending an evening, the normal English way being to sit in separate families in separate houses, each person silently occupied with a book, a paper, or a game of halma, cut off equally from the blessings of society and solitude. You may make the acquaintance of a thousand streets of middle-class English families without coming on a trace of any consciousness of citizenship, or any artistic cultivation of the senses. The condition of the men is bad enough, in spite of their daily escape into the city, because they carry the exclusive and unsocial habits of 'the home' with them into the wider world of their business. Amiable and companionable enough by nature, they are, by home training, so incredibly ill-mannered, that not even their interest, as men of business in welcoming a possible customer in every inquirer, can correct their habit of treating everybody who has not been 'introduced' as a stranger and intruder. The women, who have not even the city to educate them, are much worse: they are positively unfit for civilized intercourse – graceless, ignorant, narrow-minded to a quite appalling degree.

GEORGE BERNARD SHAW, *Plays: Pleasant and Unpleasant*

There comes out of the cloud, our house – not new to me but quite familiar, in its earliest remembrance. On the ground-floor is Peggotty's kitchen, opening into a back yard; with a pigeon-house on a pole, in the centre, without any pigeons in it; a great dog-kennel in a corner, without any dog; and a quantity of fowls that look terribly tall to me, walking about in a menacing and ferocious manner. There is one cock who gets upon a post to crow, and seems to take particular notice of me as I look at him through the kitchen window, who makes me shiver, he is so fierce. Of the geese outside the side-gate who come waddling after me with their long necks stretched out when I go that way, I dream at night; as a man environed by wild beasts might dream of lions.

Here is a long passage – what an enormous perspective I make of it! – leading from Peggotty's kitchen to the front-door. A dark store-room opens out of it, and that is a place to be run past at night; for I don't know what may be among those tubs and jars and old tea-chests, when there is nobody in there with a dimly-burning light, letting a mouldy air come out at the door, in which there is the smell of soap, pickles, pepper, candles, and coffee, all at one whiff. Then there are the two parlours; the parlour in which we sit of an evening, my mother and I and Peggotty – for Peggotty is quite our companion, when her work is done and we are alone – and the best parlour where we sit on a Sunday; grandly, but not so comfortably. There is something of a doleful air about that room to me, for Peggotty has told me – I don't know when, but apparently ages ago – about my father's funeral, and the company having their black cloaks put on. One Sunday night my mother reads to Peggotty and me in there, how Lazarus was raised up from the dead. And I am so frightened that they are afterwards obliged to take me out of bed, and show me the quiet churchyard out of the

bedroom window, with the dead all lying in their graves at rest, below the solemn moon.

There is nothing half so green that I know anywhere, as the grass of that churchyard; nothing half so shady as its trees; nothing half so quiet as its tombstones. The sheep are feeding there, when I kneel up, early in the morning, in my little bed in a closet within my mother's room, to look out at it; and I see the red light shining on the sun-dial, and think within myself, 'Is the sun-dial glad, I wonder, that it can tell the time again?' . . .

And now I see the outside of our house, with the latticed bedroom windows standing open to let in the sweet-smelling air, and the ragged old rooks'-nests still dangling in the elm-trees at the bottom of the front garden. Now I am in the garden at the back, beyond the yard where the empty pigeon-house and dog-kennel are – a very preserve of butterflies, as I remember it, with a high fence, and a gate and padlock; where the fruit clusters on the trees, riper and richer than fruit has ever been since, in any other garden, and where my mother gathers some in a basket, while I stand by, bolting furtive gooseberries, and trying to look unmoved. A great wind rises, and the summer is gone in a moment. We are playing in the winter twilight, dancing about the parlour. When my mother is out of breath and rests herself in an elbow-chair, I watch her winding her bright curls round her fingers, and straightening her waist, and nobody knows better than I do that she likes to look so well, and is proud of being so pretty.

CHARLES DICKENS, *David Copperfield*

There is a spot, 'mid barren hills,
  Where winter howls, and driving rain;
But if the dreary tempest chills,
  There is a light that warms again.

The house is old, the trees are bare,
  Moonless above bends twilight's dome;
But what on earth is half so dear –
  So longed for – as the hearth of home?

The mute bird sitting on the stone,
  The dank moss dripping from the wall,
The thorn-trees gaunt, the walks o'ergrown,
  I love them – how I love them all! . . .

A little and a lone green lane
  That opened on a common wide;
A distant, dreamy, dim blue chain
  Of mountains circling every side.

A heaven so clear, an earth so calm,
  So sweet, so soft, so hushed an air;
And, deepening still the dream-like charm,
  Wild moor-sheep feeding everywhere. . . .

EMILY BRONTË

I cannot but think it an evil sign of a people when their houses are built to last for one generation only. There is a sanctity in a good man's house which cannot be renewed in every tenement that rises on its ruins: and I believe that good men would generally feel this; and that having spent their lives happily and honourably, they would be grieved at the close of them to think that the place of their earthly abode, which had seen, and seemed almost to sympathize in, all their honour, their gladness or their suffering, – that this, with all the record it bare of them, and all of material things that they had loved and ruled over, and set the stamp of themselves upon – was to be swept away, as soon as there was room made for them in the grave; that no respect was to be shown to it, no affection felt for it, no good to be drawn from it by their children; that though there was a monument in the church, there was no warm monument in the hearth and house to them; that all that they ever treasured was despised, and the places that had sheltered and comforted them were dragged down to the dust. I say that a good man would fear this; and that, far more, a good son, a noble descendant, would fear doing it to his father's house. I say that if men lived like men indeed, their houses would be temples – temples which we should hardly dare to injure, and in which it would make us holy to be permitted to live; and there must be a strange dissolution of natural affection, a strange unthankfulness for all that homes have given and parents taught, a strange consciousness that we have been unfaithful to our fathers' honour, or that our own lives are not such as would make our dwellings sacred to our children, when each man would fain build to himself, and build for the little revolution of his life only. And I look upon those pitiful concretions of lime and clay which spring up in mildewed forwardness out of the kneaded fields about our capital – upon those thin, tottering, foundationless shells of splintered wood and imitated stone – upon those gloomy rows of formalized minuteness, alike without difference and without fellowship, as solitary as similar – not merely with the careless disgust of an offended eye, not merely with sorrow for a desecrated landscape, but with a painful foreboding that the roots of our national greatness must be deeply cankered when they are thus loosely struck in their native ground; that those comfortless and unhonoured dwellings are the signs of a great and spread-

ing spirit of popular discontent; that they mark the time when every man's aim is to be in some more elevated sphere than his natural one, and every man's past life is his habitual scorn; when men build in the hope of leaving the places they have built, and live in the hope of forgetting the years that they have lived; when the comfort, the peace, the religion of home have ceased to be felt; and the crowded tenements of a struggling and restless population differ only from the tents of the Arab or the Gipsy by their less healthy openness to the air of heaven, and less happy choice of their spot of earth; by their sacrifice of liberty without the gain of rest, and of stability without the luxury of change.

JOHN RUSKIN, *Seven Lamps of Architecture*

The Bungalows

In lofty light the towers dissolve
Of yellow elms this tranquil day,
Crumble in leisurely showers of gold
All Turneresque in bright decay.

The elms disperse their leaves upon
A nineteen-thirty builder's row
Of speculative dwellings, each
An unassuming bungalow.

Like concave shells, or shades, or shields
That guard some life or light aloof,
Like hands that cup a flame, or keep
Some frail and captured thing, each roof.

If high-pitched hopes have gone to roost
Where low-pitched roofs so smoothly slope
Perhaps these autumn rays diffuse
A deeper anodyne than hope.

Between the vast insanities
That men so cleverly invent
It may be here, it may be here,
A simulacrum of content.

Though separate only from the road
By five-foot hedge and ten-foot lawn
Each semi-isolationist
Seems almost from the world withdrawn,

Except that from a roof or two
Those thin and wand-like aerials rise
That suck like opium from the air
Bemusement for the ears and eyes.

The denizens of each hermitage,
Of 'Nellibert' and 'Mirzapore',
Bird-watchers all, in love with dogs,
Are primed with useful garden-lore:

Cabbage the emblem of their life –
Yet mauve the michaelmas-daisy glows
And under reddening apples gleams
A pearly, pure, belated rose.

Begrudging vulgar fantasy
To cheap and ordinary homes,
Discrimination might deplore
That concrete frog, those whimsy gnomes,

Nor see them as blind tribute to
The rule of dreams, or as a last
Concession to the irrational,
The old, wild, superstitious past.

The commonplace needs no defence,
Dullness is in the critic's eyes,
Without a licence life evolves
From some dim phase its own surprise:

Under those yellow-twinkling elms,
Behind those hedges trimly shorn,
As in a stable once, so here
It may be born, it may be born.

WILLIAM PLOMER

Beyond Littlestone, until after the 1914–18 war, there was no development along the coast, but then came new suburban houses placed on and above the shingle in an untidy frayed ribbon. This has developed into Greatstone, St Mary's Bay and Lydd-on-Sea (the last two named from the old villages inland). Seen across a stretch of marsh the houses take their place. At close range they are like a treeless and shrubless collection of the houses that line any by-pass out of London. They all date from the nineteen-thirties, and as a small exhibition of the popular architecture of the period they could not be bettered. Instead of backing on to a suburban electric railway they back on to the Romney, Hythe and Dymchurch miniature railway, which has its terminus at Greatstone, and beyond that there fades away the waste of shingle inland to Lydd. A few of their names indicate their character: *Hove To, Windy Cot, Midships, Galleons, Owl's Retreat, Per Mart (Percy, Martha*, perhaps), *Mount Nod, Cooparoo, Linga Longa, Sea Spray, Sea Close, Sea Wynd,*

Minarest, Thistledome (This'tle do me), Twix Us, Emohruo (Our Home,
backwards), *Ecnamor (Romance backwards), Nelande (Edna, Len*
backwards).

JOHN PIPER, *Romney Marsh*

Ewbank'd inside and Atco'd out, the English suburban resi-
dence and the garden which is an integral part of it stand trim
and lovingly cared for in the mild sunshine. Everything is in its
place. The abruptness, the barbarities of the world are far away.
There is not much sound, except perhaps the musical whirr
and clack of a mowing machine being pushed back and forth
over a neighbouring lawn and the clink of cups and saucers
and a soft footfall as tea is got ready indoors. There is not much
movement either: a wire-haired terrier lazily trotting round the
garden in a not very hopeful search for something new to
smell, and the pages of a newspaper being turned and refolded
by some leisurely individual in a deck chair. It is an almost
windless day. The leaves of the virginia creeper (*ampelopsis
veitchii*) which climbs the rough-cast wall just behind the window of the best bedroom hardly stir, and even the birds only
hop – and flutter a few feet in the air, and hop again – along the
ornamental ridge of the red-tiled roof.

Perhaps a tradesman's van is making its rounds. Perhaps at
this moment, on the other side of the screen of privet hedge and
may and laburnum which separates the garden scent of new
grass cuttings from the warm peppery scent that radiates from
asphalt pavements in summertime, the baker's boy is halting
his cart. In another moment he will push open the low wooden
gate with its embossed copper name-plate on the rail, and will
carelessly let it swing to behind him as he strides up the gravel
path with his basket of loaves on his arm. But this is only the
tradesman's entrance, and the faint squeak of the hinge and the
sound the latch makes as the gate swings back will not be very
disturbing; nor will his footsteps as he passes behind the green-
painted trellis with the rockery at its foot towards the kitchen
door at the side of the house.

Inside it is more peaceful still. The sunlight coming through
the bottle glass of the front door falls in irregular blotches on
the coconut mat made by blind ex-service men, on the fumed
oak hatstand and on the wall-rack holding a variety of walking

sticks collected on summer holidays, including one with a spiked ferrule and a sprig of edelweiss cut in the wood below the handle. These blotches of sunlight make the narrow hall seem rather dark by contrast. It smells faintly of furniture polish and somewhat more faintly of the American cloth of which the hood of a folding perambulator is made, a perambulator for which there is really not enough room in the hall, as the visitor will soon discover if he steps too confidently past the foot of the stairs. The far part of the hall is lighter because a door is slightly ajar, and through it there is a glimpse of the drawing room: a sofa with loose covers in flowered chintz, faded with much laundering, cream paint, the corner of a piano with framed photographs on it and a bay window with leaded panes, the centre part opening to the ground and leading down a couple of steps to the bright garden.

J. M. RICHARDS, *The Castles on the Ground*

O Happy Dogs of England

O happy dogs of England
Bark well as well you may
If you lived anywhere else
You would not be so gay.

O happy dogs of England
Bark well at errand boys
If you lived anywhere else
You would not be allowed to
     make such an infernal noise.

STEVIE SMITH

There is, in every English home, a certain room in which may be found the queerest accumulation of disused objects, covered with the dust and rust of time: boxes of old clothes which will never see the light again, pathetic gas-brackets which have had to give way to electric fittings, disembowelled armchairs which are not worth repairing, old cradles which will never see another baby, guns which have ceased to shoot, golf clubs which have given up clubbing, and banjos which have broken their strings and lost their voice. Coming across such a medley of rubbish, the outsider will scratch his head and ask himself why on earth the lady of the house, whom he knows to be most efficient and orderly, does not get rid of these things to make use of the room for some intelligible purpose. He may even, if he is sufficiently intimate with her, raise the question as a modest contribution to the welfare of the family, trusting that this suggestion will meet with complete approval. Need I add that his audacity will not obtain the reward it so well deserves? It will be useless for him to try and bolster up utilitarian arguments with Christian ones, and to say that these discarded objects might have given pleasure to others, if they had been given away before they had been destroyed by lying idle too long. He will be properly snubbed and told to mind his own business: 'I do not know what your continental housewife would do with such things, but I have kept them and I am going to keep them, because they may come in useful some day.' The stranger will be wise to let it rest at that, for if he hints that fashions have changed and that it is not likely that gas will come into its own again, he may run into worse trouble.

This kind of box-room or lumber-room is not only characteristic of the English home but of all English institutions. There is a positive objection in England to anything that looks like 'scrapping'. Past traditions and titles and costumes are essentially respectable; they may have become useless, but if they do no good they can certainly do no harm, and then – who knows? – there is an attractive element of doubt as to their future destiny. The English, for these reasons, preserve their seventeenth century University gowns, their Warden of the Cinque Ports, and such obsolete ministerial titles as Chancellor of the Duchy of Lancaster and Lord Privy Seal. They retain the mediaeval edict according to which no Member of Parliament is allowed to resign, and the old institution of the Chiltern Hundreds, and they neutralize any inconvenience caused by the first of these rules by allowing any Member no longer in agreement with his Party to apply for a Stewardship in this institution. The Beefeaters make a good show on the day of the Opening of Parliament, and the Guy Fawkes carnival enlivens the gloom of our November climate:

> I sing a doleful tragedy,
>   Guy Fawkes, that Prince of Sinisters,
> Who once blew up the House of Lords,
>   The King and all his Ministers;
> That is, he would have blown 'em up,
>   And folks won't soon forget him:
> His will was good to do the deed,
>   That is, if they'd ha' let him.

EMILE CAMMAERTS, *Discoveries in England*

Does it often happen to people who have been in a new house only a year and a half, to feel as if they had never lived anywhere else? How it may be with others I know not, but my own little new-built house is so restful, so satisfying, so kindly sympathetic, that so it seems to me.

In some ways it is not exactly a new house, although no building ever before stood upon its site. But I had been thinking about it for so many years, and the main block of it and the whole sentiment of it were so familiar to my mind's eye, that when it came to be a reality I felt as if I had already been living in it a good long time. And then, from the way it is built it does not stare with newness; it is not new in any way disquieting to the eye; it is neither raw nor callow. On the contrary, it almost gives the impression of a comfortable maturity of something like a couple of hundred years. And yet there is nothing sham-old about it; it is not trumped-up with any specious or fashionable devices of spurious antiquity; there is no pretending to be anything that it is not – no affectation whatever.

But it is designed and built in the thorough and honest spirit of the good work of old days, and the body of it, so fashioned and reared, has, as it were, taken to itself the soul of a more ancient dwelling-place. The house is not in any way a copy of any old building, though it embodies the general characteristics of the older structures of its own district.

Everything about it is strong and serviceable, and looks and feels as if it would wear and endure for ever. All the lesser permanent fittings are so well thought out and so thoroughly made that there is hardly anything that can possibly get out of order; the house is therefore free from the petty worry and dislocation of comfort so commonly caused by the weakness or inefficiency of its lesser parts, and from the frequent disturbance occasioned by workmen coming to do repairs.

Internal fittings that are constantly seen and handled, such as window-fastenings, hinges, bolts and door-latches, are specially designed and specially made, so that they are in perfect proportion, for size, weight, and strength, to the wood and iron-work to which they are related. There are no random choosings from the ironmonger's pattern-book; no clashing of styles, no meretricious ornamentation, no impudence of cast-iron substi-

tute for honest hand-work, no moral slothfulness in the pro-
viding of all these lesser finishings. It takes more time, more
trouble; it may even take a good deal of time and trouble, but
then it is just right, and to see and know that it is right is a daily
reward and a never-ending source of satisfaction.

GERTRUDE JEKYLL, *Home and Garden*

They are awfully funereal, those ornaments of the close of the
last century – tall, gloomy horse-hair chairs, mouldy Turkey
carpets, with wretched druggets to guard them, little cracked
sticking-plaster miniatures of people in *tours* and pig-tails over
high-shouldered mantelpieces, two dismal urns on each side of
a lanky sideboard, and in the midst a queer twisted receptacle
for worn-out knives with green handles. Under the sideboard
stands a cellaret that looks as if it held half a bottle of currant
wine, and a shivering plate-warmer that never could get any
comfort out of the wretched old cramped grate yonder. Don't
you know in such houses the grey gloom that hangs over the
stairs, the dull-coloured old carpet that winds its way up the
same, growing thinner, duller and more threadbare, as it
mounts to the bedroom floors? There is something awful in the
bedroom of a respectable old couple of sixty-five. Think of the
old feathers, turbans, bugles, petticoats, pomatum-pots, spen-
cers, white satin shoes, false fronts, the old flaccid, boneless
stays tied up in faded ribbon, the dusky fans, the old forty-
years-old baby-linen, the letters of Sir George when he was
young, the doll of poor Maria, who died in 1803, Frederick's
first corduroy breeches, and the newspaper which contains
the account of his distinguishing himself at the siege of
Seringapatam. All these lie somewhere, damp and squeezed
down into glum old presses and wardrobes. At that glass the
wife has sat many times these fifty years; in that old morocco
bed her children were born. Where are they now? Fred, the
brave captain, and Charles, the saucy colleger; there hangs a
drawing of him done by Mr Beechey, and that sketch by
Cosway was the very likeness of Louis before . . .

They call that room the nursery still, and the little wicket still
hangs at the upper stairs: it has been there for forty years – *bon
Dieu!* Can't you see the ghosts of little faces peering over it? I

132

wonder whether they get up in the night as the moonlight shines into the blank, vacant old room, and play there solemnly with little ghostly horses, and the spirits of dolls, and tops that turn and turn but don't hum.

WILLIAM MAKEPEACE THACKERAY, *Men's Wives*

In England every man *ought* to own a garden. It's meant to be that way, you feel it immediately.

HENRY MILLER

And now to sum up as to a garden. Large or small, it should look both lively and rich. It should be well fenced from the outside world. It should by no means imitate either the wilfulness or the wildness of Nature, but should look like a thing never to be seen except near a house. It should, in fact, look like a part of the house.

WILLIAM MORRIS, *Hopes and Fears for Art*

The taste of the English in the cultivation of land, and in what is called landscape-gardening, is unrivalled. They have studied nature intently, and discover an exquisite sense of her beautiful forms and harmonious combinations.

Those charms, which in other countries she lavishes in wild solitudes, are here assembled round the haunts of domestic life. They seem to have caught her coy and furtive graces, and spread them, like witchery, about their rural abodes.

Nothing can be more imposing than the magnificence of English park scenery. Vast lawns that extend like sheets of vivid green, with here and there clumps of gigantic trees, heaping up rich piles of foliage; the solemn pomp of groves and woodland glades, with the deer trooping in silent herds across them; the hare, bounding away to the covert; or the pheasant, suddenly bursting upon the wing; the brook, taught to wind in natural meanderings, or expand into a glassy lake; the sequestered pool, reflecting the quivering trees, with the yellow leaf sleeping on its bosom, and the trout roaming fearlessly about its limpid waters, while some rustic temple or sylvan statue, grown green and dark with age, gives an air of classic sanctity to the seclusion.

These are but a few of the features of park scenery; but what most delights me is the creative talent with which the English decorate the unostentatious abodes of middle life. The rudest habitation, the most unpromising and scanty portion of land, in the hands of an Englishman of taste, becomes a little paradise.

With a nicely discriminating eye, he seizes at once upon its capabilities, and pictures in his mind the future landscape. The sterile spot grows into loveliness under his hand; and yet the operations of art which produce the effect are scarcely to be perceived. The cherishing and training of some trees; the cautious pruning of others; the nice distribution of flowers and plants of tender and graceful foliage; the introduction of a green slope of velvet turf; the partial opening to a peep of blue distance, or silver gleam of water: all these are managed with a delicate tact, a pervading yet quiet assiduity, like the magic touchings with which a painter finishes up a favourite picture.

WASHINGTON IRVING, *The Sketch Book: Rural Life in England*

Cottage Gardens

Some of these cottages in summer-time really approach something of that Arcadian beauty which is supposed to prevail in the country. Everything, of course, depends upon the character of the inmates. The dull tint of the thatch is relieved here and there by great patches of sillgreen which is religiously preserved as a good herb, though the exact ailments for which it is 'good' are often forgotten. One end of the cottage is often completely hidden with ivy, and woodbine grows in thickest profusion over the porch. Near the door there are almost always a few cabbage-rose trees, and under the windows grow wallflowers and hollyhocks, sweet peas, columbine and sometimes the graceful lilies of the valley. The garden stretches in a long strip from the door, one mass of green. It is enclosed by thick hedges, over which the dog-rose grows, and the wild convolvulus will blossom in the autumn. Trees fill up every available space and corner – apple trees, pear trees, damsons, plums, bullaces – all varieties. The cottages seem to like to have at least one tree of every sort. These trees look very nice in the spring when the apple blossom is out, and again in the autumn when the fruit is ripe. Under the trees are gooseberry bushes, raspberries and numbers of currants. The patches are divided into strips producing potatoes, cabbage, lettuce, onions, radishes, parsnips; in this kitchen produce, as with the fruit, they like to possess a few of all kinds. There is generally a great bunch of rhubarb. In odd corners there are sure to be a few specimens of southernwood, mugwort, and other herbs; not for use, but from adherence to the old customs. The old people thought much of these 'yjerbs', so they must have some too. as well as a little mint and similar potherbs. In the windows you may see two or three geraniums, and over the porch a wicker cage, in which the 'ousel cock, with orange-tawny bill' pours out his rich, melodious notes. There is hardly a cottage without its captive bird, or tame rabbit, or mongrel cur, which seems as much attached to his master as more high-bred dogs to their owners.

RICHARD JEFFERIES

A London 'Garden'

Some London houses have a melancholy little plot of ground behind them, usually fenced in by four high whitewashed walls and frowned upon by stacks of chimneys, in which there withers on from year to year a crippled tree, that makes a show of putting forth a few leaves late in autumn, when other trees shed theirs, and drooping in the effort, lingers on all crackled and smoke-dried till the following season, when it repeats the same process, and perhaps if the weather be particularly genial, even tempts some rheumatic sparrow to chirrup in its branches. People sometimes call these dark yards 'gardens'; it is not supposed that they were ever planted, but rather that they are pieces of unreclaimed land, with the withered vegetation of the original brick-field. No man thinks of walking in this desolate place, or of turning it to any account. A few hampers, half-a-dozen broken bottles, and such-like rubbish, may be thrown there when the tenant first moves in, but nothing more; and there they remain till he goes away again, the damp straw taking just as long to moulder as it thinks proper, and mingling with the scanty box, and stunted everbrowns, and broken flower-pots, that are scattered mournfully about – a prey to 'blacks' and dirt.

CHARLES DICKENS, Nicholas Nickleby

Of all miserable habitations an English house in very hot or very cold weather is the worst.

SYDNEY SMITH

The parade, labour, skill, and paraphernalia required to maintain and manage an English fire are bewildering to a foreigner. There are the grate, and the ornamented fender, and the rug before the hearth; the steel shovel, tongs, and poker that are kept for beauty not use; and the steel poker, tongs, and shovel that are to be used. Need I say that the foreigner always undertakes to employ the wrong poker and is detested accordingly? Then there is the handsome coal-box that stands by the fireside, and the ugly coal-scuttle which the maid carries in and out to replenish the former. Matches, waste-paper, bundles of kindling wood *ad libitum*, and the first issue thereof is smoke. Presently there comes flame, and then, after many hours of manipulation, heat is generated. Not much heat, but still enough to make one wish for more. Meanwhile, the fire consumes the coals with a fiendish disregard of their price per sack. By way of revenge, I presume, everybody who enters the room gives the fire a savage poke . . . There is no other institution in England so troublesome, vexatious, unsatisfactory, and ungrateful as an English fire; but the people love it, and praise it, and shiver round it, as if it were a fire from heaven.

STEPHEN FISKE, Photographs by an American

In nothing is the English genius for domesticity more notably declared than in the institution of this festival – almost one may call it so – of afternoon tea. Beneath simple roofs, the hour of tea has something in it of the sacred; for it marks the end of domestic work and worry, the beginning of restful, sociable evening. The mere chink of cups and saucers tunes the mind to happy repose. I care nothing for your five o'clock tea of modish drawing-rooms, idle and wearisome like all else in which that world has part; I speak of tea where one is *at home* in quite another than the worldly sense. To admit mere strangers to your tea-table is profanation; on the other hand, English hospitality has here its kindliest aspect; never is a friend more welcome than when he drops in for a cup of tea.

GEORGE GISSING, *Private Papers of Henry Ryecroft*

Throughout the whole of England the drinking of tea is general. You have it twice a day and, though the expense is considerable, the humblest peasant has his tea twice a day just like the rich man: the total consumption is immense. The high cost of sugar or molasses, of which large quantities are required, does not prevent this custom being a universal one, to which there are no exceptions.

FRANÇOIS DE LA ROCHEFOUCAULD

I pray thee, gentle Renny dear,
   That thou wilt give to me,
With cream and sugar temper'd well,
   Another dish of tea.

Nor fear that I, my gentle maid,
   Shall long detain the cup,
When once unto the bottom I
   Have drunk the liquor up.

Yet hear, at last, this mournful truth,
   Nor hear it with a frown,
Thou canst not make the tea so fast
   As I can gulp it down.

SAMUEL JOHNSON

It would be impossible to love the English as I do, without being sensitive to the appeal of tea. It may take a while to get used to it, though. But there is no valid reason why the Path should stop at the fire, water and air Trials: to become initiated into English life you must pass through the tea trial as well. I have been, in the past, to all sorts of more or less dreary tea parties, and always with the most disheartening results: at every tea party I lost a little of my self-respect: even when those parties were attended by my favourite girls. You understand, of course, that I am now talking in the past sense, the passé imparfait. This is what happened: I was walking along Oxford Street, direction Marble Arch. This is my favourite walk, on account of the shop windows, the French windows, the French cinemas, the ex-convicts and the ten-shilling whores (incidentally, they don't call themselves whores but naughty girls – probably for the same reason that the butchers call themselves purveyors of first-class meat). It was drizzling and my hands felt cold. I can't exactly tell how it happened, but suddenly a strange feeling formulated itself in my mind: all of a sudden I said to myself: 'I am dying for a cup of tea.' You must have heard that phrase before. Anyway, I have, and I hated it. It was the phrase that made me feel disgusted with Millie and Billie and Daisy and Dorothy; with the United Kingdom and the British Empire. Tea has always been torture to me: it exalted my Uranus, pouring fiery oil all over my trines and sextiles. It was like the battle-cry of the enemy. And now, without the least preparation, I found myself standing half-wittedly in front of a Lyons shop and muttering to myself that stupid and infuriating phrase: 'I am dying for a cup of tea.'

Anyway, to cut a long story short, I walked into the tea-shop all by myself (without having a date!), sat down at a table crowded with orphans and their families, and ordered a pot of tea and two buttered scones. I even specified that it must be Indian tea! Can you beat it, Joey? The most amazing part about this self-inflicted tea was that I actually enjoyed it! With every sip I took England became clearer to me. 'A most refreshing drink,' I whispered to my inner self as I poured myself the third cup. I let my gaze wander about the place. Five o'clock. London, and perhaps the whole English-speaking world, is full of tea drinkers at this time of day. Tea is being drunk in twelve thousand Lyons and ABC shops. In Buckingham Palace. In the army and on the battleships before Gibraltar. In the gaols, too, I am told. A deluge of tea every day. Enough to flood the Yangtze River. The orphans were having a wonderful time gorging on tea and 'French' pastry tasting like vanishing cream. A most refreshing drink. Outside it was raining. The place smelled of rain and Burberrys and Players tobacco. With every sip of tea I swallowed the atmosphere of London. At a certain moment, which some day I will be able to recapture, the whole of London became plausible to me. It lasted only a second, but during that brief moment of time I succeeded in pinning London down. London ceased to be an immense monstrosity where one can be alone and comfortable: it became the logical outgrowth of a tea-drinking nation. London was no longer a fairy-city, there was a definite raison d'être for it. It had a purpose, a mission. London revealed itself to me in the clatter of tea things. I can't tell you what the revelation was, I can hardly tell you what effect it had on me. I came out of the place in a daze. It was still raining. The street was in a mist. The people looked isolated in their mackintoshes, like phantoms. The cops, motionless and tall, like Easter Island statues. Fire hydrants and traffic lights. Cockney accent. Everything focused into familiarity. I must have known the city for a thousand years. For the first time I felt that I had a claim on London, after all. I can no longer be expelled without pain. Once more I have struck root. I have added a new set of gestures to my mannerism. Maybe one of these days I will wear an umbrella. Or become a member of the Church of England. Or even a gentleman.

ALFRED PERLES, letter to Henry Miller, 1946

Most edifying is their talk at table, when they cut their gigantic roast beef, and ask you with an earnest face what sort of a slice you would like, whether thick or thin, whether an inside or an outside piece, whether fat or lean. Heaven preserve any Christian man from their sauces, which consist either of one-third flour and two-thirds butter, or according to the taste of the cook, one-third butter and two-thirds flour. Heaven preserve everybody from their plain vegetables! which they boil in water, just as God made them, and then set them on the table. More horrible even than the cooking in England are their toasts and their set dinner-speeches, when the table cloth is removed and the ladies get up and leave the table; and in their stead so many bottles of port wine are brought in – since they consider the absence of the fair sex is thus best replaced (I say the fair sex, for Englishwomen deserve the appellation).

HEINRICH HEINE, *English Fragments*

I cannot relish their food; they eat meat half raw; the vegetables are never boiled enough to be soft; and everything is insipid except the bread which is salt, bitter and disagreeable. The cheese and butter were more to my taste. Generous wines are inordinately dear, and no others to be procured. What you find at the inns is in general miserably bad.

ROBERT SOUTHEY, *Letters from England*

I take advantage of this letter to curse, as I must, the abominable 'ox-tail' soup. Fi, the horror! There is also 'coffee plain per cup', a ghastly mixture of dried chicory and milk! Most horrible! And the gin! Extract of sewage. The fish is horrible, sole, mackerel, whiting etc. . . . all soft, sticky, and flabby. They give you fried sole with a piece of lemon, as large as a duck's heart; meat, vegetables, fruit, all good, but too dear. Warm beer.

PAUL VERLAINE, letter to Edmond Lepelletier

The bread I eat in London is a deleterious paste, mixed up with chalk, alum, and bone-ashes; insipid to the taste, and destructive to the constitution. The good people are not ignorant of this adulteration; but they prefer it to wholesome bread, because it is whiter than the meal of corn: thus they sacrifice their taste and their health, and the lives of their tender infants, to a most absurd gratification of a misjudging eye; and the miller, or the baker, is obliged to poison them and their families, in order to live by his profession. The same monstrous depravity appears in their veal, which is often bleached by repeated bleedings, and other villainous arts, till there is not a drop of juice left in the body, and the poor animal is paralytic before it dies; so void of all taste, nourishment, and savour, that a man might dine as comfortably on a white fricassee of kid-skin gloves, or chip hats from Leghorn.

As they have discharged the natural colour from their bread, their butchers'-meat and poultry, their cutlets, ragouts, fricassees, and sauces of all kinds; so they insist upon having the complexion of their pot-herbs mended, even at the hazard of their lives. Perhaps, you will hardly believe they can be so mad as to boil their greens with brass half-pence, in order to improve their colour; and yet nothing is more true. Indeed, without this improvement in the colour, they have no personal merit. They are produced in an artificial soil, and taste of nothing but the dunghills, from whence they spring. . . .

It must be owned that Covent Garden affords some good fruit; which, however, is always engrossed by a few individuals of overgrown fortune, at an exorbitant price; so that little else than the refuse of the market falls to the share of the community; and that is distributed by such filthy hands, as I cannot look at without loathing. It was but yesterday that I saw a dirty barrow-bunter in the street, cleaning her dusty fruit with her own spittle; and, who knows but some fine lady of St James's parish might admit into her delicate mouth those very cherries, which had been rolled and moistened between the filthy, and, perhaps, ulcerated chops of a St Giles's huckster. I need not dwell upon the pallid, contaminated mash, which they call strawberries; soiled and tossed by greasy paws through twenty baskets crusted with dirt; and then presented with the worst milk, thickened with the worst flour, into a bad likeness of cream: but the milk itself should not pass unanalysed, the produce of faded cabbage-leaves and sour draff, lowered with hot water, frothed with bruised snails, carried through the streets in open pails, exposed to foul rinsings, discharged from doors and windows, spittle, snot, and tobacco-quids from foot-passengers, overflowings from mud-carts, spatterings from coach-wheels, dirt and trash chucked into it by roguish boys for the joke's-sake, the spewings of infants, who have slabbered in the tin-measure, which is thrown back in that condition among the milk, for the benefit of the next customer; and, finally, the vermin that drops from the rags of the nasty drab that vends this precious mixture, under the respectable denomination of milk-maid. . . .

TOBIAS SMOLLETT, *Humphrey Clinker*

It is commonly said, even by the English themselves, that English cooking is the worst in the world. It is supposed to be not merely incompetent, but also imitative, and I even read quite recently, in a book by a French writer, the remark: 'The best English cooking is, of course, simply French cooking.'

Now that is simply not true. As anyone who has lived long abroad will know, there is a whole host of delicacies which it is quite impossible to obtain outside the English-speaking countries. No doubt the list could be added to, but here are some of the things that I myself have sought for in foreign countries and failed to find.

First of all, kippers, Yorkshire pudding, Devonshire cream, muffins and crumpets. Then a list of puddings that would be interminable if I gave it in full: I will pick out for special mention Christmas pudding, treacle tart and apple dumplings. Then an almost equally long list of cakes: for instance, dark plum cake (such as you used to get at Buzzard's before the war), short-bread and saffron buns. Also innumerable kinds of biscuit, which exist, of course, elsewhere, but are generally admitted to be better and crisper in England.

Then there are the various ways of cooking potatoes that are peculiar to our own country. Where else do you see potatoes roasted under the joint, which is far and away the best way of cooking them? Or the delicious potato cakes that you get in the north of England? And it is far better to cook new potatoes in the English way – that is, boiled with mint and then served with a little melted butter or margarine – than to fry them as is done in most countries.

Then there are the various sauces peculiar to England. For instance, bread sauce, horse-radish sauce, mint sauce and apple sauce; not to mention redcurrant jelly, which is excellent with mutton as well as with hare, and various kinds of sweet pickle, which we seem to have in greater profusion than most countries.

What else? Outside these islands I have never seen a haggis, except one that came out of a tin, nor Dublin prawns, nor Oxford marmalade, nor several other kinds of jam (marrow jam and bramble jelly, for instance), nor sausages of quite the same kind as ours.

Then there are the English cheeses. There are not many of them but I fancy that Stilton is the best cheese of its type in the world, with Wensleydale not far behind. English apples are also outstandingly good, particularly the Cox's Orange Pippin.

And finally, I would like to put in a word for English bread. All the bread is good, from the enormous Jewish loaves flavoured with caraway seeds to the Russian rye bread which is the colour of black treacle. Still, if there is anything quite as good as the soft part of the crust from an English cottage loaf (how soon shall we be seeing cottage loaves again?) I do not know of it.

No doubt some of the things I have named above could be obtained in continental Europe, just as it is possible in London to obtain vodka or bird's nest soup. But they are all native to our shores, and over huge areas they are literally unheard of.

GEORGE ORWELL, *Evening Standard*, 15 December 1946

FUN AND GAMES

The populace has its amusements and very rude ones, such as throwing dead dogs and cats and mud at passers-by on certain festival days. Another amusement which is very inconvenient to passers-by is football. For this game a leather ball filled with air is used, and is kicked about with the feet. In cold weather you sometimes see a score of rascals in the streets kicking at a ball, and they will break panes of glass and smash the windows of coaches, and also knock you down without the slightest compunction; on the contrary, they will roar with laughter. Another great pleasure of the people is the ringing of bells, and it is a source of great delight to them whenever an opportunity of doing this presents itself. I do not suppose there is a country where bell-ringing is brought to such an art as it is here, where bells are always in chime and in harmony. You will scarcely believe me when I tell you that, with six or eight bells of various tones, in an hour's time a good bell-ringer can ring out more than a thousand different peals and chimes.

The English are very fond of a game they call cricket. For this purpose they go into a large open field, and knock a small ball about with a piece of wood. I will not attempt to describe this game to you, it is too complicated; but it requires agility and skill, and everyone plays it, the common people and also men of rank. Sometimes one county plays against another county. The papers give notice of these meetings beforehand, and, later, tell you which side has come off victorious. Spectators crowd to these games when they are important.

CÉSAR DE SAUSSURE, *Letters*, 1725

There are better games, as games. Frequently there is no decision at all in cricket, sometimes scarcely a beginning. But it is on rainy days that the charm of the game has been known to work its most subtle spells for those who play country cricket, away from the bricks and mortar of Kennington and Leeds (both much beloved in their places). The vacant and rural field is shrouded in mist as you walk through the entrance-gate hoping against hope. There is a sound of footsteps on the wooden pavilion; perhaps there'll be play after all. Then the clouds are suddenly pulled apart, and the sun changes the grass to a field of jewels. And men in white appear from nowhere, and soon two little mounds of sawdust are placed at each end of the wicket and bowlers sometimes lose volition like boys on a slide, and the bat sends forth its ineffectual thud; while in adjacent trees the birds make busy noises, and aloft in the blue sky there are great castles on cliffs of clouds, and burning lakes. These things all belong to the game as much as the implements, the technical achievement, and the 'result'.

NEVILLE CARDUS, *English Cricket*

At Lord's

The nostalgia for cricket seems a kind of madness to those who have it not. They come late in life or from foreign parts willing to be instructed in the mysteries and, being instructed, are still inexpressibly bored; they cannot understand what we see in the game. The answer is that it is not the game only that we see, but childhood and youth, and peace of mind in the recollection of enduring things:

> For the field is full of shades as I near the shadowy coast,
> And a ghostly batsman plays to the bowling of a ghost,
> And I look through my tears on a soundless-clapping host
> As the run-stealers flicker to and fro,
>   To and fro:–
> O my Hornby and my Barlow long ago!

CHARLES MORGAN

Of the games I played at Cambridge, soccer has remained a wind-swept clearing in the middle of a rather muddled period. I was crazy about goalkeeping. In Russia and the Latin countries, that gallant art had been always surrounded with a halo of singular glamour. Aloof, solitary, impassive, the crack goalie is followed in the streets by entranced small boys. He vies with the matador and the flying ace as an object of thrilled adulation. His sweater, his peaked cap, his kneeguards, the gloves protruding from the hip pocket of his shorts, set him apart from the rest of the team. He is the lone eagle, the man of mystery, the last defender. Photographers, reverently bending one knee, snap him in the act of making a spectacular dive across the goal mouth to deflect with his fingertips a low, lightning-like shot, and the stadium roars in approval as he remains for a moment or two lying full length where he fell, his goal still intact.

But in England, at least in the England of my youth, the national dread of showing off and a too grim preoccupation with solid teamwork were not conducive to the development of the goalie's eccentric art. This at least was the explanation I dug up for not being oversuccessful on the playing fields of Cambridge. Oh, to be sure, I had my bright, bracing days – the good smell of turf, that famous inter-Varsity forward, dribbling closer and closer to me with the new tawny ball at his twinkling toe, then the stinging shot, the lucky save, its protracted tingle. . . . But there were other, more memorable, more esoteric days, under dismal skies, with the goal area a mass of black mud, the ball as greasy as a plum pudding, and my head racked with neuralgia after a sleepless night of verse-making. I would fumble badly – and retrieve the ball from the net. Mercifully the game would swing to the opposite end of the sodden field. A weak, weary drizzle would start, hesitate, and go on again. With an almost cooing tenderness in their subdued croaking, dilapidated rooks would be flapping about a leafless elm. Mists would gather. Now the game would be a vague bobbing of heads near the remote goal of St John's or Christ's, or whatever college we were playing. The far, blurred sounds, a cry, a whistle, the thud of a kick, all that was perfectly unimportant and had no connection with me. I was less the keeper of a soccer goal than the keeper of a secret. As with folded arms I leant my back against the left goalpost, I enjoyed the luxury of closing my eyes, and thus I would listen to my heart knocking and feel the blind drizzle on my face and hear, in the distance, the broken sounds of the game, and think of myself as of a fabulous exotic being in an English footballer's disguise, composing verse in a tongue nobody understood about a remote country nobody knew. Small wonder I was not very popular with my teammates.

VLADIMIR NABOKOV, *Speak, Memory*

Bell-ringing in England is known among ringers as 'the exercise', rather as the rearing and training of pigeons is known among the pigeon fraternity as 'the fancy'. It is a classless folk art which has survived in the church despite all arguments about doctrine and the diminution of congregations. In many a church when the parson opens with the words 'Dearly beloved brethren, the Scripture moveth us in sundry places . . .' one may hear the tramp of the ringers descending the newel stair into the refreshing silence of the graveyard. Though in some churches they may come in later by the main door and sit in the pew marked 'Ringers Only', in others they will not be seen again, the sweet melancholy notes of 'the exercise' floating out over the Sunday chimney-pots having been their contribution to the glory of God. So full of interest and technicality is the exercise that there is a weekly paper devoted to it called *The Ringing World*.

A belfry where ringers are keen has the used and admired look of a social club. There, above the little bit of looking-glass in which the ringers slick their hair and straighten their ties before stepping down into the outside world, you will find blackboards with gilded lettering proclaiming past peals rung for hours at a stretch. In another place will be the rules of the tower written in a clerkly hand. A charming Georgian ringers' rhyme survives at St Endellion, Cornwall, on a board headed with a picture of ringers in knee-breeches:

> We ring the Quick to Church and dead to Grave,
> Good is our use, such usage let us have
> Who here therefore doth Damn, or Curse or Swear,
> Or strike in Quarrel thogh no Blood appear,

Who wears a Hatt or Spurr or turns a Bell
Or by unskilful handling spoils a Peal,
Shall Sixpence pay for every single Crime
'Twill make him careful 'gainst another time.
Let all in Love and Friendshiip hither come,
Whilst the shrill Treble calls to Thundering Tom,
And since bells are our modest Recreation
Let's Rise and Ring and Fall to Admiration.

Many country towers have six bells. Not all these bells are medieval. Most were cast in the seventeenth, eighteenth or nineteenth centuries when change-ringing was becoming a country exercise. And the older bells will have been re-cast during that time, to bring them into tune with the new ones. They are likely to have been again re-cast in modern times, and the ancient inscription preserved and welded on to the re-cast bell. Most counties have elaborately produced monographs about their church bells. The older bells have beautiful lettering sometimes, as at Somerby, and South Somercotes in Lincolnshire, where they are inscribed with initial letters decorated with figures so that they look like illuminated initials from old manuscripts interpreted in relief on metal. The English love for Our Lady survived in inscriptions on church bells long after the Reformation, as did the use of Latin. Many eighteenth- and even early nineteenth-century bells have Latin inscriptions. A rich collection of varied dates may be seen by struggling about on the wooden cage in which the bells hang among the bat-droppings in the tower.

Many local customs survive in the use of bells. In some places a curfew is rung every evening; in others a bell is rung at five in the morning during Lent. Fanciful legends have grown up about why they are rung, but their origin can generally be traced to the divine offices. The passing bell is rung differently from district to district. Sometimes the years of the deceased are tolled, sometimes the ringing is three strokes in succession followed by a pause. There are instances of the survival of prayers for the departed where the bell is tolled as soon as the news of the death of a parishioner reaches the incumbent.

Who has heard a muffled peal and remained unmoved? Leather bags are tied to one side of the clapper and the bells ring alternately loud and soft, the soft being an echo, as though in the next world, of the music we hear on earth.

I make no apology for writing so much about church bells. They ring through our literature, as they do over our meadows and roofs and few remaining elms. Some may hate them for their melancholy, but they dislike them chiefly, I think, because they are reminders of Eternity. In an age of faith they were messengers of consolation.

JOHN BETJEMAN, *The Collins Guide to Parish Churches*

The first of all English games is making money. That is an all-absorbing game; and we knock each other down oftener in playing at that, than at football, or any other roughest sport: and it is absolutely without purpose; no one who engages heartily in that game ever knows why. Ask a great money-maker what he wants to do with his money – he never knows. He doesn't make it to do anything with it. He gets it only that he *may* get it. 'What will you make of what you have got?' you ask. 'Well, I'll get more,' he says. Just as at cricket, you get more runs. There's no use in the runs, but to get more of them than other people is the game. So all that great foul city of London there, – rattling, growling, smoking, stinking, – a ghastly heap of fermenting brickwork, pouring out poison at every pore, – you fancy it is a city of work? Not a street of it! It is a great city of play; very nasty play and very hard play, but still play.

JOHN RUSKIN, *The Crown of Wild Olive*

Taverns and Inns

We dined at an excellent inn at Chapel-house, where he expatiated on the felicity of England in its taverns and inns, and triumphed over the French for not having, in any perfection, the tavern life. 'There is no private house' (said he) 'in which people can enjoy themselves so well, as at a capital tavern. Let there be ever so great plenty of good things, ever so much grandeur, ever so much elegance, ever so much desire that every body should be easy; in the nature of things it cannot be: there must always be some degree of care and anxiety. The master of the house is anxious to entertain his guests; the guests are anxious to be agreeable to him: and no man, but a very impudent dog indeed, can as freely command what is in another man's house, as if it were his own. Whereas, at a tavern, there is a general freedom from anxiety. You are sure you are welcome: and the more noise you make, the more trouble you give, the more good things you call for, the welcomer you are. No servants will attend you with the alacrity which waiters do, who are incited by the prospect of an immediate reward in proportion as they please. No, Sir; there is nothing which has yet been contrived by man, by which so much happiness is produced as by a good tavern or inn.' He then repeated, with great emotion, Shenstone's lines:

> 'Whoe'er has travell'd life's dull round,
> Wher'er his stages may have been,
> May sigh to think he still has found
> The warmest welcome at an inn.'

JAMES BOSWELL, *Life of Samuel Johnson*

The humour in pubs varies greatly, but all forms are to be enjoyed. Farmers have a picturesque humour of their own. At the Feathers in Ludlow I heard one of them describe how he had shot at several rabbits that day and had failed to bag them. 'Plenty o' room round 'em, ain't there?' said another. But country people have a lot of time on their hands for solitary brooding, with the result that, once they get going, they easily become the world's leading non-stop talkers; and they are liable to record episodes the comedy in which may not appeal to outsiders. For example, I heard the following account of a dialogue the other day, which stuck in my mind because of the gusto with which it was told and the hilarity with which it was received:

"Ow's your turnips?' ses ee. "Ow's my turnips?' ses I. 'Yes,' ses ee, "ow's your turnips?' 'Well,' ses I, 'come to that, 'ow's yourn?' "Ow's mine?' ses ee. 'Yes,' ses I, "ow's yourn? "Oh,' ses ee, 'they beant too bad.' 'No more,' ses I, 'ain't mine.' (Laughter.) 'No more ain't mine,' ses I. (More laughter.)

The loudest shout of mirth I ever heard in a pub greeted a tale told by a poacher, who in the course of his nightly prowling had come across a gamekeeper lying in a pool of blood, the victim of an accident. 'Was ee dead?' asked a yokel during the thrilled hush that fell upon the company at the bar. 'Dead!' echoed the poacher: 'Ee'd blown 'is bloody 'ed off! Laff? I thought I should ha' died o' laffin'!'

HESKETH PEARSON, This Blessed Plot

Those entering the Saloon Bar of The Midnight Bell from the street came through a large door with a fancifully frosted glass pane, a handle like a dumb-bell, a brass inscription *'Saloon Bar and Lounge'* and a brass adjuration to Push. Any one temperamentally so wilful, careless, or incredulous as to ignore this friendly admonition was instantly snubbed, for this door actually would only succumb to Pushing. Nevertheless hundreds of temperamental people nightly argued with this door and got the worst of it.

Given proper treatment, however, it swung back in the most accomplished way, and announced you to the Saloon Bar with a welcoming creak. The Saloon Bar was narrow and about thirty feet in length. On your right was the bar itself, in all its bottly glitter, and on your left was a row of tables set against a comfortable and continuous leather seat which went the whole length of the bar. At the far end the Saloon Bar opened out into the Saloon Lounge. This was a large, square room, filled with a dozen or so small, round, copper-covered tables. Around each table were three or four white wicker armchairs, and on each table there lay a large stone ash-tray supplied by a whisky firm. The walls were lined with a series of prints depicting moustached cavalrymen in a variety of brilliant uni-

forms; there was a fireplace with a well-provided fire; the floor was of chessboard oil-cloth, broken by an occasional mat, and the whole atmosphere was spotless, tidy, bright, and a little chilly. This was no scene for the brawler, but rather for the principled and restrained drinker, with his wife. In here and in the Saloon Bar, The Midnight Bell did most of its business – the two other bars (the Public and the Private) being dreary, seatless, bareboarded structures wherein drunkenness was dispensed in coarser tumblers and at a cheaper rate to a mostly collarless and frankly downtrodden stratum of society. The Public Bar could nevertheless be glimpsed by a customer in the Saloon Bar, and as the evening wore on it provided the latter with an acoustic background of deep mumbling and excited talk without which its whole atmosphere would have been lost

– without which, indeed, the nightly drama of the Saloon Bar
would have been rather like a cinematograph drama without
music. . . .

PATRICK HAMILTON, *2000 Streets Under the Sky*

Darts

A dart-board consists of two narrow concentric circles intersected by twenty segments.

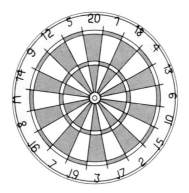

Each of these twenty segments is numbered according to a fascinating mathematical formula, which I am unable to work
out, so that a high number so far as possible is next to a low
number, and so that the even and odd numbers are properly
balanced round the board. Any dart that lodges in the segment
called 20 counts 20; but if it lodges in the part of the segment
intersected by the narrow outer circle it counts twice twenty,
and if in the part intersected by the narrow inner circle it counts
three times twenty. So the outer ring is called the Double Ring,
and the inner ring is called the Treble. In the very centre of the
board there is a tiny circle (counting 50) surrounded by another
circle counting 25; but these are rarely used.

In ordinary darts you must score exactly 301, beginning and
finishing in the double ring. Thus the perfect player could win
a game in two hands of three darts (the players throw three
darts each, in turn) by scoring thus:

First dart, *double* 20	– 40
Second dart, treble 20	– 60
Third dart, treble 20	– 60
	← Other man throws
Fourth dart, treble 20	– 60
Fifth dart, treble 19	– 57
Sixth dart, *double* 12	– 24
	301

Nothing counts at all until you have got a dart into the double ring to begin with, and your last dart has got to be a double that brings your score to 301 exactly. This is why my perfect player threw his fifth dart at the treble 19, instead of at the treble 20. If he had failed to switch from even numbers to odd ones he would have been in a mess. Suppose he had gone on at the treble 20, and got it. This would have left him 21, to make the exact 301; and it is not possible to score 21 in a double ring, for it is an odd number. He would then have had to waste another dart in getting a single one (leaving him double 10) or a single three (leaving him double 9) or a single five (leaving him double 8) or a single seven (leaving him double 7) or etc.

The first player to achieve his 301, throwing in turns and tossing for start, is the winner.

T. H. WHITE, *England Have My Bones*

The English drinking establishments, properly speaking, merit the description, 'outside it is fine, but inside it is poor' (refrain from an operetta). The front is in wood the colour of mahogany, but with great copper ornaments. To the height of a man the windows are filled with coloured glass, flowers, birds, etc., like Duval's. You enter by a terribly thick door kept half open by a formidable strap, which (the door) catches you in the back after having knocked off your hat. The interior is quite small, a zinc slab covers the mahogany counter, beside which either standing or perched on very high, very narrow stools drink, smoke, and talk through their noses well-dressed gentlemen, disagreeable, poor porters and drivers as swollen and hairy as ours. Behind the counter are waiters with their shirt sleeves turned up, or young women, generally pretty, with untidy hair, elegantly dressed in bad taste, who are playfully prodded by a finger, a stick, or an umbrella to the accompaniment of coarse laughter and apparently coarse words which do not seem to shock them.

PAUL VERLAINE, *London Sketches*

Clubs

We were walking early one morning down the Strand; the rising sun whitened the spires of London. Suddenly out of the blue my companion, a Scotsman attached to one of the great dailies, said as if to himself, 'They have large ears, they have long feet, they have no fear, they live in secret; but they are known to each other; and they cannot understand defeat.' Dimly, I knew that he was talking about the governors of England. I did not take it all in at once. 'Where do they live?' I asked. 'In their clubs and in the hunting districts.' I cannot say why I guessed that he was talking about the men who govern England, men who live in secret and who cannot understand defeat. Probably it was the last description that gave me the dim clue. And 'their clubs' decided it. To these men, governments with their prime ministers who are mere puppets may come and go, one thing remains which is permanency.

So they live in their clubs? From that morning I began to take an interest in their clubs. I found out some facts which may be diverting. . . .

Now the great thing about an English club is its exclusiveness. One might think that it is the duty of every member to make it as hard as possible for anyone else to become a member. I forgot to mention the fact that a would-be member has to be examined by members of the committee of the club to which he aspires on the neutral ground of another club. This may be the cause of a member trying to exclude all others from membership. He feels that he has passed all tests, and has therefore acquired in some mysterious way a distinction which he is not supposed to share. Otherwise it would diminish his club's exclusiveness. A club must be above all things select.

Freedom is another attribute. If one's house, thanks to the Fabianism of the late English government, has ceased to be one's castle, one's club remains inviolable. The story goes – and I do not think that it is apocryphal – that a lady, growing anxious toward nightfall, called up her husband's club.

'Is my husband there?' she asked. 'No, madam,' was the prompt reply.

'What do you mean, "No, Madam"? I have not told you my name.'

'There never ain't no 'usbands 'ere,' the well-trained flunky replied. They live in secret.

London is the home of clubs proper. By 'proper' is meant the club as described above. White's; Boodles; St James's; the Travellers'; the Bachelors'; the Beefsteak; the Royal Yacht Club; and Oxford and Cambridge, senior and junior (I have never heard of a senior), are proper clubs. They are oases from the many who make a desert of life. They magnify one's importance and are factories of self-esteem. They are ends in themselves. Therefore they have nothing to do with charities and that sort of thing. They are not formed for the maintenance of hospitals, giving boys annual holidays, or contributing to the cure of disease. On the contrary, they are refuges from the invasion which too much good fellowship brings. That is, perhaps, why they are nodes of silence. Members are not expected to recognize one another in the better-class clubs. You may talk on the stairs; but only when you are entertaining a guest.

OLIVER ST JOHN GOGARTY, *A Weekend in the Middle of the Week*

The English love hobbies. Almost every Englishman with any spare time at all has a hobby, and it is almost impossible to guess from his profession or appearance what that hobby is likely to be. It may be stamp-collecting or carpentry or digging up Roman pottery, or simply digging up his own potatoes. Gardening is no doubt the most usual hobby of all, and there are men and women everywhere, both in town and country, who have that happy knack of making things grow which is summed up in the vivid phrase 'green fingers'. You can hear them talking 'shop' in trains and over garden fences, and at all the innumerable flower shows of the spring and summer, from

the famous one at Chelsea to the small local affairs which cause such deadly rivalry among all kinds of gardeners. Sometimes people join a club so as to share their particular passion with others: the Photographic Club, the Archaeological, or whatever it may be. But there are plenty of happy solitaries, busily building a model sailing-ship out of matches or gloating over their collection of foreign railway-tickets, who feel no need of company or encouragement. The hobby is enough in itself.

A hobby may seem a trivial matter, but to an Englishman it is often of more absorbing interest than his profession or trade. He may have had his job in life forced upon him; his hobby he has chosen for himself, and it sometimes reveals a good deal about his character. How highly the English rate their hobbies you can see from the fact that they are listed as a matter of course by practically all the eminent men and women whose biographies appear in *Who's Who*.

MONICA REDLICH, *Everyday England*

The Diehards

We go, in winter's biting wind,
On many a short-lived winter day,
With aching back but willing mind
To dig and double-dig the clay.

All in November's soaking mist
We stand and prune the naked tree,
While all our love and interest
Seem quenched in blue-nosed misery.

We go in withering July
To ply the hard incessant hoe;
Panting beneath the brazen sky
We sweat and grumble, but we go.

We go to plead with grudging men,
And think it is a bit of luck
When we can wangle now and then
A load or two of farmyard muck.

What do we look for as reward?
Some little sounds, and scents, and scenes:
A small hand darting strawberry-ward,
A woman's apron full of greens.

A busy neighbour, forced to stay
By sight and smell of wallflower-bed;
The plum-trees on an autumn day,
Yellow, and violet, and red.

Tired people sitting on the grass,
Lulled by the bee, drugged by the rose,
While all the little winds that pass
Tell them the honeysuckle blows.

The sense that we have brought to birth
Out of the cold and heavy soil,
These blessed fruits and flowers of earth
Is large reward for all our toil.

RUTH PITTER

Walking

English people are great walkers. This, perhaps, is the reason they give so much importance to the quality of their shoes. Their shoes – strong, comfortable, and yet elegant – invite you to cover long distances on foot.

The better-class Englishman takes his walk no matter what the weather may be. Rain does not keep him indoors; rather has it a particular attraction for this type of Englishman. He will say to you: It is refreshing – and invite you to accompany him. If you are equipped with clothes as well made as his, you will agree on returning that you enjoyed the walk.

And, in fact, as English shoes and raincoats do not let water through, a few miles in the rain puts you right for the whole afternoon. Naturally, if the sun is shining, it is so much the better. The unmistakably English scenery is, however, that offered you by a misty day, which blots out the tints, making people and objects evanescent. Having come from the South, you will never forget an immersion in this spectral atmosphere.

Words and Expressions

walking – *a passeggio.*
to cover long distances on foot – *percorrere grandi distanze a piedi.*
takes his walk, no matter what the weather – *fa la sua passeggiata con qualsiasi tempo.*
rain does not keep him indoors – *la pioggia non lo trattiene in casa.*

do not let water through – *non fanno passar l'acqua.*
puts you right – *vi mettono a posto.*
so much the better – *tanto meglio.*
so much the worse – *tanto peggio.*
the unmistakably English scenery – *il paesaggio incon-*
fondibilmente inglese.
which blots out the tints – *che smorza le tinte.*

GUIDO PUCCIO, *Customs on the Other Side of the Channel*

The Derby

The day was exceptionally beautiful; the charming sky was spotted over with little idle-looking, loafing, irresponsible clouds; the Epsom Downs went swelling away as greenly as in a coloured sporting-print, and the wooded uplands, in the middle distance, looked as innocent and pastoral as if they had never seen a policeman or a rowdy. The crowd that spread itself over this immense expanse was as rich a representation of human life off its guard as one need see. One's first fate after arriving, if one is perched upon a coach, is to see the coach guided, by means best known to the coachman himself, through the tremendous press of vehicles and pedestrians, introduced into a precinct roped off and guarded from intrusion save under payment of a fee, and then drawn up alongside of the course, as nearly as possible opposite the grand stand and the winning post. Here you have only to stand up in your place – on tip-toe, it is true, and with a good deal of stretching – to see the race fairly well. But I hasten to add that seeing the race is indifferent entertainment. In the first place you *don't* see it, and in the second – to be Irish on the occasion of a frolic – you perceive it to be not much worth the seeing. It may be fine in quality, but in quantity it is inappreciable. The horses and their jockeys first go dandling and cantering along the course to the starting-point, looking as insubstantial as sifted sunbeams. Then there is a long wait, during which, of the sixty thousand people present (my figures are imaginary), thirty thousand declare positively that they have started, and thirty thousand as positively deny it. Then the whole sixty thousand are suddenly resolved into unanimity by the sight of a dozen small jockey heads whizzing along a very distant sky-line. In a shorter space of time than it takes me to write it, the whole thing is before you, and for the instant it is anything but beautiful. A dozen furiously revolving arms – pink, green, orange, scarlet, white – whacking the flanks of as many straining steeds; a glimpse of this, and the spectacle is over. The spectacle, however, is of course an infinitesimally small part of the purpose of Epsom and the interest of the Derby. The finer vibration resides presumably in having money on the affair.

When the Derby Stakes had been carried off by a horse of which I confess I am barbarous enough to have forgotten the name, I turned my back to the running, for all the world as if I too were largely 'interested', and sought entertainment in looking at the crowd. The crowd was very animated; that is the most succinct description I can give of it. The horses of course had been removed from the vehicles, so that the pedestrians were free to surge against the wheels and even to a certain extent to scale and overrun the carriages. This tendency became most pronounced when, as the mid-period of the day was reached, the process of lunching began to unfold itself and every coach top to become the scene of a picnic. From this moment, at the Derby, demoralization begins. I was in a position to observe it, all around me, in the most characteristic forms. The whole affair, as regards the conventional rigidities I spoke of a while since, becomes a *dégringolade*. The shabbier pedestrians bustle about the vehicles, staring up at the lucky mortals who are perched in a kind of tormentingly near empyrean – a region in which dishes of lobster-salad are passed about and champagne-corks cleave the air like celestial meteors. There are nigger-minstrels and beggars and mountebanks and spangled persons on stilts and gipsy matrons, as genuine as possible, with glowing Oriental eyes and dropping their *h*'s; these last offer you for sixpence the promise of everything genteel in life except the aspirate. On a coach drawn up beside the one on which I had a place, a party of opulent young men were passing from stage to stage of the higher beatitude with a zeal which excited my admiration. They were accompanied by two or three young ladies of the kind that usually shares the choicest pleasures of youthful British opulence – young ladies in whom nothing has been neglected that can make a complexion superlative. The whole party had been drinking deep, and one of the young men, a pretty lad of twenty, had in an indiscreet moment staggered down as best he could to the ground. Here his cups proved too many for him, and he collapsed and rolled over. In plain English he was beastly drunk. It was the scene that followed that arrested my observation. His companions on the top of the coach called down to the people herding under the wheels to pick him up and put him away inside. These people were the grimiest of the rabble, and a couple of men who looked like coal-heavers out of work undertook to handle this hapless youth. But their task was difficult; it was impossible to imagine a young man more drunk. He was a mere bag of liquor – at once too ponderous and too flaccid to be lifted. He lay in a helpless heap under the feet of the crowd – the best intoxicated young man in England. His extemporized chamberlains took him first in one way and then in another; but he was like water in a sieve. The crowd hustled over him; every one wanted to see; he was pulled and shoved and fumbled. The spectacle had a grotesque side, and this it was that seemed to strike the fancy of the young man's comrades. They had not done lunching, so they were unable to bestow upon the incident the whole of that consideration which its high comicality deserved. But they did what they could. They looked down very often, glass in hand, during the half-hour that it went on, and they stinted neither their generous, joyous laughter nor their appreciative comments. Women are said to have no sense of humour; but the young ladies with the complexions did liberal justice to the pleasantry of the scene. Toward the last indeed their attention rather flagged; for even the best joke suffers by reiteration, and when you have seen a stupefied young man, infinitely bedusted, slip out of the embrace of a couple of clumsy roughs for the twentieth time, you may very properly suppose that you have arrived at the furthest limits of the ludicrous.

HENRY JAMES, *English Hours*

Hunting

The chase of the fox is a very favourite diversion in this kingdom, and is nowhere pursued with such ardour and intrepidity. Both our dogs and horses are confessedly superior to those of any other country. The instant the fox finds he is pursued, he flies towards his hole; and finding it stopped, which is always carefully done before the chase begins, he has recourse to his speed and his cunning for safety. He does not double and measure his ground back like the hare, but continues his course straight forward before the hounds, with great strength and perseverance. Both dogs and horses, particularly the latter, have frequently fallen victims to the ardour of the pursuit, which has sometimes continued for upwards of fifty miles without the smallest intermission, and almost at full speed.* As the scent of the fox is very strong, the dogs follow with great

alacrity and eagerness, and have been known to keep up a constant chase for eight or ten hours together; and it is hard to say whether the spirited eagerness of the hounds, the ardour of the horses, or the enthusiasm of the hunters is most to be admired. The fox is the only one of the party which has the plea of necessity on his side; and it operates so strongly, that he often escapes the utmost efforts of his pursuers, and returns to his hole in safety. The smell of his urine is so offensive to the dogs, that it sometimes proves the means of his escape from them. When all his shifts have failed him, and he is at last overtaken, he then defends himself with great obstinacy and fights in silence till he is torn in pieces by the dogs.

* Mr Charles Turner's hounds hunted at Ayreyholm, near Hurworth in the county of Durham, and found the noted old fox CAESAR, which made an extraordinary chase. After a round of four miles, he led to Smeaton, through Hornby and Appleton; then back again to

Hornby, Worsetmoor, Piersburgh, Limpton, Craythorn, Middleton, Hilton, Seamer, Newby, Marton, Ormsby; then upon Hambleton through Kirkleatham park, Upleatham, Skelton, and Kelton. Mr Turner tired three horses; and only three hounds were in pursuit, when he thought it proper to call them off, it being near five in the evening. The chase was upwards of fifty miles.

THOMAS BEWICK, *A History of Quadrupeds*

A score or two of gentlemen riding full speed down a hill nearly as steep as the roof of a house, where one false step must inevitably send horse and rider to certain death, is an object to be seen nowhere but in England.

WILLIAM COBBETT

When I first came to Waltham Cross in the winter of 1859–1860, I had almost made up my mind that my hunting was over. I could not then count upon an income which would enable me to carry on an amusement which I should doubtless find much more expensive in England than in Ireland. I brought with me out of Ireland one mare, but she was too light for me to ride in the hunting-field. As, however, the money came in, I very quickly fell back into my old habits. First one horse was bought, then another, and then a third, till it became established as a fixed rule that I should not have less than four hunters in the stable. Sometimes when my boys have been at home I have had as many as six. Essex was the chief scene of my sport, and gradually I became known there almost as well as though I had been an Essex squire, to the manner born. Few have investigated more closely than I have done the depth, and breadth, and water-holding capacities of an Essex ditch. It will, I think, be accorded to me by Essex men generally that I have ridden hard. The cause of my delight in the amusement I have never been able to analyse to my own satisfaction. In the first place, even now, I know very little about hunting, – though I know very much of the accessories of the field. I am too blind to see hounds turning, and cannot therefore tell whether the fox has gone this way or that. Indeed all the notice I take of hounds is not to ride over them. My eyes are so constituted that I can never see the nature of a fence. I either follow some one, or ride at it with the full conviction that I may be going into a horse-pond or a gravel-pit. I have jumped into both the one and the other. I am very heavy, and have never ridden expensive horses. I am also now old for such work, being so stiff that I cannot get on to my horse without the aid of a block or bank. But I ride still after the same fashion, with a boy's energy, determined to get ahead if it may possibly be done, hating the roads, despising young men who ride them, and with a feeling that life can not, with all her riches, have given me anything better than when I have gone through a long run to the finish, keeping a place, not of glory, but of credit, among my juniors.

ANTHONY TROLLOPE, *Autobiography*

Does anyone go fishing nowadays, I wonder? Anywhere within a hundred miles of London there are no fish left to catch. A few dismal fishing clubs plant themselves in rows along the banks of canals, and millionaires go trout-fishing in private waters round Scotch hotels, a sort of snobbish game of catching hand-reared fish with artificial flies. But who fishes in mill streams or moats or cow-ponds any longer? Where are the English coarse fish now? When I was a kid every pond and stream had fish in it. Now all the ponds are drained and when the streams aren't poisoned with chemicals from factories they're full of rusty tins and motorbike tyres.

GEORGE ORWELL, *Coming Up For Air*

Shooting

Pteryplegia, or the Art of Shooting Flying Birds was written by Mr George Markland, who in 1726 was the first man to recognize the possibility of slaying a pheasant on the wing. Prior to this date the proper way to slay a pheasant was when it was sitting down.

Sport is not the act of killing. Killing is a very mere business, the prerogative of butchers and people who want something to eat. It is practised by the lower orders, Aborigines and animals. Tigers kill, and hawks do, but for the disgraceful purpose of eating their victims. Sport is unknown among animals, Aborigines, the lower orders and butchers. If sport were merely the act of killing, it would be sport to be a butcher or an Aborigine, and this is manifestly not the case.

When you are throwing pebbles at a biscuit tin on the sea-shore, and often hitting it, you will either go farther away to make your shots or else set up a smaller tin if such be available. You will handicap yourself. When the committee finds that the fourteenth hole was done by old Mr Sloworm in two under bogey, they will lay out a new bunker or take the tee-box farther back. They will put difficulties in his way. When the magician finds that juggling with two balls has become so easy as to be second nature, he will either begin to juggle with four balls or give it up altogether, and anybody who has ever taken up knitting will know that no sooner had he mastered the plain and purl than he was anxious to match himself against a rope stitch or something like that.

It is this instinct, the instinct to back oneself against the difficulties, that is the basis of all sports. The fisherman finds that it is relatively easy to catch trout on the worm, so he handicaps himself (increases the difficulty which has to be overcome) by determining to catch trout on a hook ornamented with a piece of rubber tube in the likeness of a worm. The slayer of foxes becomes bored by murdering them with a gun, so he expends eight thousand pounds a year in training dogs to do it in a much more complicated manner. The shooter, able to butcher any number of sitting rabbits by creeping up to them while they are feeding in the evening, stands up and waves his arms to make them run.

The greater the difficulty, the greater the pleasure in overcoming it. If there is no difficulty, there is no pleasure, and it is thus that difficulty or handicap has become the essence of sport, and that which distinguishes it from simple killing.

Retired colonels are apt to voice this truth unwittingly, when they say that a sitting shot is 'unsporting' because it does not give the quarry a 'sporting chance'. What they mean is that the sitting shot is unsporting because it does not give them a sporting chance of missing (thus adding to their pleasure if they hit), but somehow or other the colonels have got the roles mixed up, and for them the rabbit appears to be enjoying the sport which is laboriously offered to it by the colonel. Except for this slight confusion of personalities, the colonels are quite right.

Nearly all animals are beautiful and interesting while they are alive. This beauty is gravely diminished by death, because they are no longer able to move their beauty then, and motion is a great part of loveliness. Thus the young boy who shoots his first rabbit and stands holding it while the soft hazel eye of this quite harmless (except to farmers) and pleading herbivore moves through terror and agony to glaze: this boy, for that first time, realizes that he has committed hideous murder, the sin against the Holy Ghost. A little chaffing by his seniors, the habit of a few more emulative slaughters, and a certain inherent beastliness still common to the human mind, will in the end render him impervious to such sensations – provided that he has made a good shot. When he murdered his first rabbit, possibly a sitting shot, he was horrified by the realization that he had destroyed beauty. This horrible realization will soon be dulled by custom, *provided that in destroying that beauty he can at the same time congratulate himself upon having created another beauty, the beautiful shot.*

This is what lies at the bottom of the taboo about sitting shots. It is a taboo created in order to save the shooter pain. If he destroys a sitting pheasant he has merely destroyed beauty, and some twinge of that young boy's emotion, which he once was, will return to plague the inventor; but if he destroys it in its full glory on the wing, he can smother this remorse under the other beauty of his successful aim.

T. H. WHITE, *Burke's Steerage*

'What a fine day it is. Let us go out and kill something.' The old reproach against the English.

FRANCIS KILVERT

THE SEA

The Coast – Norfolk

As on the highway's quiet edge
He mows the grass beside the hedge,
The old man has for company
The distant, grey, salt-smelling sea,
A poppies' field, a cow and calf,
The finches on the telegraph.

Across his faded back a hone
He slowly, slowly scythes alone
In silence of the wind-soft air
With ladies' bedstraw everywhere,
With whitened corn, and tarry poles
And far-off gulls like risen souls.

FRANCES CORNFORD

Tuesday 13 July [1875]. This morning after breakfast I started to
walk to Bembridge through Sandown and Yaverland. The
morning was blue and lovely with a warm sun and fresh breeze
blowing from the sea and the Culver Downs. As I walked from
Shanklin to Sandown along the cliff edge I stopped to watch
some children bathing from the beach directly below. One
beautiful girl stood entirely naked on the sand, and there as she
half sat, half reclined sideways, leaning upon her elbow with
her knees bent and her legs and feet partly drawn back and up,
she was a model for a sculptor, there was the supple slender

171

waist, the gentle dawn and tender swell of the bosom and the budding breasts, the graceful rounding of the delicately beautiful limbs and above all the soft and exquisite curves of the rosy dimpled bottom and broad white thigh. Her dark hair fell in thick masses on her white shoulders as she threw her head back and looked out to sea. She seemed a Venus Anadyomene fresh risen from the waves.

I missed the road by the windmill on the height and went too far round to the right, but at last returning by the Cross Roads I came to Bembridge. Bosomed amongst green, pretty cottages peeped through the thick foliage and here and there a garden shone brilliant with flowers. A long beautiful road, dark, green and cool and completely overarched with trees, led towards the sea and in a high meadow the haymakers in their white shirt sleeves, the dark horses and the high loaded waggon stood out clear against the brilliant blue waters of the Channel. Farther on a broad and beautiful avenue led down to the water's edge. The trees were chiefly sycamore and ash, and high and thickly overarching they cast a twinkling chequering shadow upon the ground, a perpetual restless flicker of dancing leaves that in the sun and sea wind moved ceaselessly quivering. Only two or three children were moving up and down in the chequering sunlight and shadow. At the end of the avenue the bright blue sea was framed in a perfect round low arch of dark foliage, and passing under the arch I came out upon an open terrace from which a pretty winding path wandered amongst the woods which fringe the shore and sweep down to the water's edge. Spithead was full of great ships black and monstrous. The Channel Fleet had come in the day before and was lying off the opposite shore. The sun shone bright on the green slopes and woods and white houses of St Helens across the smooth blue harbour of Brading, a woman sat solitary under the trees looking across the sea to the Hampshire coast, and the only sounds that broke the peaceful stillness were the rustling of the firs and poplars overhead and the clapping of the white sail of a pilot boat as it flapped idly from the yard in the soft sea breeze.

FRANCIS KILVERT, *Diaries*

Mr and Mrs Stephen Grosvenor-Smith
(He manages a Bank in Nottingham)
Have come to Sandy Cove for thirty years
And now they think the place is going down.
   'Not what it was, I'm very much afraid.
Look at that little mite with *Attaboy*
Printed across her paper sailor hat.
Disgusting, isn't it? Who *can* they be,
Her parents, to allow such forwardness?'
   The Browns, who thus are commented upon,
Have certainly done very well indeed.
The elder children bringing money in,
Father still working; with allowances
For this and that and little income-tax,
They probably earn seven times as much
As poor old Grosvenor-Smith. But who will grudge
Them this, their wild, spontaneous holiday?
The morning paddle, then the mystery tour
By motor-coach inland this afternoon.
For that old mother what a happy time!
At last past bearing children, she can sit
Reposeful on a crowded bit of beach.
A week of idleness, the salty winds
Play in her greying hair; the summer sun
Puts back her freckles so that Alfred Brown
Remembers courting days in Gospel Oak
And takes her to the Flannel Dance tonight.
But all the same they think the place 'Stuck up'
And Blackpool, next year – if there *is* a next.
   And all the time the waves, the waves, the waves
Chase, intersect and flatten on the sand
As they have done for centuries, as they will
For centuries to come, when not a soul
Is left to picnic on the blazing rocks,
When England is not England, when mankind
Has blown himself to pieces. Still the sea,
Consolingly disastrous, will return
While the strange starfish, hugely magnified,
Waits in the jewelled basin of a pool.

JOHN BETJEMAN, from 'Beside the Seaside'

Blackpool. A wonderful, clean place. The Old Theatre is now a bingo hall. There are three piers, the North (this was built first), the South and the Central. The illuminations go on for two months from September to October. It was in Blackpool that the first tram service started. The Great Theatre was built in 1894. It must be the prettiest theatre in the country. There were 230 theatres built by the same man (Coliseum, Palladium, Victoria Palace, Hippodrome etc.) and only about eighteen remain. The circus is magnificent. It is the only permanent circus in Britain.

We visited a boarding house (now called a guest house) which cost £5 a day. There are streets and streets of these boarding houses in Blackpool. In June pensioners come, in July and August families do. Usually they come from the same town together, settle down in the same boarding house; sometimes streets are full of the same people from the same villages. They bring with them their own atmosphere. When the illuminations are over, the boarding house people go for their holidays to the Bahamas, Miami, Spain. The boarding houses are full of cheap things, tasteless but clean. No bugs any more. Tea and coffee, though, are poured out from kettles, the milk already mixed in.

We visited a rock factory. There are about ten to twelve rock factories in Blackpool. The one we visited had twenty workers, amongst them sixteen women – a cheap labour force. They export a lot to Saudi Arabia of all places. Blackpool rock is superior rock. Alan quoted Johnson about the factory: 'No man is more innocently employed than when making money.'

We also visited the illumination factory which is the only one in the country. Approximately one hundred people work here, amongst them one Hungarian and one Pole. In 1956 more than 1,000 Hungarians came to Blackpool. One man, called Mr Eliot, made the whole factory, he designed everything and said they did not work for profit. The illuminations began before the First World War. They have cost about £800,000 but at least there are eight million people who are drawn to visit Blackpool to see the illuminations and they spend about £50 million. This is a wonderful deal. This year the new showpieces are the saucy postcards as illumination items.

In Blackpool everything serves low tastes.

Alan used to come to Blackpool on horse back, riding along the sand from Lytham.

In the old days people used to stay in the Hotel Metropol; we are now in the Imperial Hotel. Labour Party leaders usually stay here for the Conference.

Alan said that in Victorian England the servants used to iron the newspapers before passing them to the owner of the house.

The Blackpool pleasure beach was overrun by fortune tellers, gipsies, old fashioned fairs, but now there are American influences as well.

Blackpool was compared with Paris thus: 'By comparison with Blackpool, Paris is sweet and Sodom a Paradise.'

EVA TAYLOR, *A Life with Alan* (A. J. P. Taylor)

Holiday Memory

August Bank Holiday. A tune on an ice-cream cornet. A slap of sea and a tickle of sand. A fanfare of sunshades opening. A wince and whinny of bathers dancing into deceptive water. A tuck of dresses. A rolling of trousers. A compromise of paddlers. A sunburn of girls and a lark of boys. A silent hullabaloo of balloons.

I remember the sea telling lies in a shell held to my ear for a whole harmonious, hollow minute by a small, wet girl in an enormous bathing-suit marked 'Corporation Property'.

I remember sharing the last of my moist buns with a boy and a lion. Tawny and savage, with cruel nails and capacious mouth, the little boy tore and devoured. Wild as seed-cake, ferocious as a hearth-rug, the depressed and verminous lion nibbled like a mouse at his half a bun, and hiccupped in the sad dusk of his cage.

I remember a man like an alderman or a bailiff, bowlered and collarless, with a bag of monkey-nuts in his hand, crying 'Ride 'em, cowboy!' time and again as he whirled in his chairoplane giddily above the upturned laughing faces of the town girls bold as brass and the boys with padded shoulders and shoes sharp as knives; and the monkey-nuts flew through the air like salty hail.

Children all day capered or squealed by the glazed or bashing sea, and the steam-organ wheezed its waltzes in the threadbare playground and the waste lot, where the dodgems dodged, behind the pickle factory. . . .

There was cricket on the sand, and sand in the sponge cake, sand-flies in the watercress, and foolish, mulish, religious donkeys on the unwilling trot. Girls undressed in slipping tents of propriety; under invisible umbrellas, stout ladies dressed for

the male and immoral sea. Little naked navvies dug canals; children with spades and no ambition built fleeting castles; wispy young men, outside the bathing huts, whistled at substantial young women and dogs who desired thrown stones more than the bones of elephants. Recalcitrant uncles huddled over luke ale in the tiger-striped marquees. Mothers in black, like wobbling mountains, gasped under the discarded dresses of daughters who shrilly braved the goblin waves. And fathers, in the once-a-year sun, took fifty winks. Oh, think of all the fifty winks along the paperbagged sand. . . .

I remember the patient, laborious, and enamouring hobby, or profession, of burying relatives in sand.

I remember the princely pastime of pouring sand, from

cupped hands or buckets, down collars and tops of dresses; the shriek, the shake, the slap.

I can remember the boy by himself, the beachcombing lone-wolf, hungrily waiting at the edge of family cricket; the friend-less fielder, the boy uninvited to bat or to tea.

I remember the smell of sea and seaweed, wet flesh, wet hair, wet bathing-dresses, the warm smell as of a rabbity field after rain, the smell of pop and splashed sunshades and toffee, the stable-and-straw smell of hot, tossed, tumbled, dug, and trod-den sand, the swill-and-gaslamp smell of Saturday night, though the sun shone strong, from the bellying beer-tents, the smell of the vinegar on shelled cockles, winkle-smell, shrimp-smell, the dripping-oily backstreet winter-smell of chips in newspapers, the smell of ships from the sun-dazed docks round the corner of the sand-hills, the smell of the known and paddled-in sea moving, full of the drowned and herrings, out and away and beyond and further still towards the antipodes that hung their koala-bears and Maoris, kangaroos, and boom-erangs, upside down over the backs of the stars.

DYLAN THOMAS, *Quite Early One Morning*

3 September [1797]. Walked on the beach, watching the retiring and returning waves, and attending to the bursting thunder of the surge.

Afterwards stood on a fortified point below the castle, imme-diately and high over the beach, commanding a vast marine horizon, with a long tract of the French coast, a white line bounding the blue waters. Below, on the right, Dover curves picturesquely along the sea-bay; the white and green cliffs ris-ing closely over it, except near the castle, where they give place to hills, that open to a green valley, with enclosures and a pretty village, beyond which it winds away. The most grand and striking circumstances, as we stood on the point, were – the vast sea-view – the long shades on its surface of soft green, deepening exquisitely into purple; but, above all, that downy tint of light blue, that sometimes prevailed over the whole scene, and even faintly tinged the French coast, at a distance. Sometimes, too, a white sail passed in a distant gloom, while all between was softly shadowed; the cliffs above us broken and encumbered with fortifications; the sea viewed beyond them, with vessels passing from behind; the solemn sound of the tide, breaking immediately below, and answered, as it were, at measured intervals, along the whole coast; this circumstance inexpressibly grand; the sound more solemn and hollow than when heard on the beach below. A fleet of merchantmen, with a convoy, passed and spread itself over the channel.

Afternoon. – Walked towards Shakespeare's Cliff; the fleet still in view. Looked down from the edge of the cliffs on the fine red gravel margin of the sea. Many vessels on the horizon and in mid-channel. The French coast, white and high, and clear in the evening gleam. Evening upon the sea becoming melancholy, silent and pale. A leaden-coloured vapour rising upon the horizon, without confounding the line of separation; the ocean whiter, till the last deep twilight falls, when all is one gradual, inseparable, undistinguishable, grey.

19 October [1811]. Left Steephill. Sailed from Cowes in the Southampton packet, about half-past five; the Naiad frigate lying before the town. What particularly struck me in the passage was, not only the sun actually appearing to set in the sea, but the splendid amber light, left upon that long level perspective of waters, and the vessels upon it at various distances, seeming dark on this side, and marking out its extent to the eye. The grace and majesty of an anchored ship, too, lying with her stern to the eye, though at less distance, is indescribable; showing all her shrouds and yards lessening, like a pyramid, as they rise upon the light. How tranquil and grand the scene lay, beneath the gradually deepening shade! Still the dark shores and stately vessels kept their dignity upon the fading waters. How impressive the silence, and then how according the solemn strain, that died upon the waves from unseen and distant bugles, like a song of peace to the departing day! Another of those measured portions that make up our span of life, was gone; everyone who gazed upon this scene, proud or humble, was a step nearer to the grave – yet none seemed conscious of it. The scene itself, great, benevolent, sublime – powerful, yet silent in its power – progressive and certain in its end, steadfast and full of a sublime repose: the scene itself spoke of its CREATOR.

ANNE RADCLIFFE

You ask for my impressions of this place, so you shall have a few. The day after I arrived they were far from favourable, but variety has crept in since then. In the morning I remember I had some conversation with an Italian ice-cream man. 'We're having a wicked summer,' he remarked as the rain began to patter on his white drill coat, and he turned his back to the sea, which had gone the colour of dirty pewter. In the distance a few old people hobbled into the shelters along the Marina, and a wet blanket of mist and rain was drawn by the wind over the eastern and western heights, over the great blocks of Victorian barracks and the walls of the abbey. In the park the trees were weeping floods of tears, and an empty tram was making a hurried and noisy exit from the High Street.

No wonder the French family, day trippers, felt that England was hopeless. They too retired to a shelter to consume the food and drink they had brought with them (for everybody knows that in England eatable food as a rule is unobtainable, except at exorbitant prices, and drink forbidden, except at odd hours); they wrung the water out of their berets and wondered if it had wetted their cameras, and then, with their mouths full, began to calculate, not without difficulty, since English money is so complicated, how they might avoid spending anything at all.

'Don't tell me it's raining,' said a meek little man with the quietest irony. He was about to step out of the post office into the deluge. The English are said to take their pleasures sadly, but is it not even more important that they take their misfortunes cheerfully? On days like that one is reminded of Taine's remark that *'le fond du caractère anglais, c'est l'absence de bonheur.'*. . .

One afternoon I walked over to Kingstrand. There was a strong wind that dotted the sea with curly white waves, rather stylized. The sea was streaked with loud blues and greens, and the wind prevented the fishing-boats, which were turned against it, from making headway. With their dusky cigar-brown sails they dipped and fluttered, struggling like moths in glue. Everything was movement, nothing was progress. The waves broke and whitened as far as the eye could see, the sailing-boats rocked and tilted and got no further, the grass on the cliff streamed along the ground but stuck to its roots. At

Kingstrand the villas below the cliff were not yet opened for the summer, and the shuttered beach-huts, their paint faded by sun and salt, had an air of secrecy, as though a crime had been committed in one of them. Between the houses and the huts there is a flat of shingle a hundred yards wide, and here great masses of pink valerian have run wild. It was all in flower, dancing against the clean buff shingle and the peacocking sea.

I came back a different way from the way I went, and passed through that curious region known as the Ness. The first thing you come to is one of those military follies that occasionally adorn the English landscape, a city of derelict huts solidly built of concrete but now overgrown with elder-bushes and nettles, a refuge for tramps, courting couples, and idle boys on Sunday afternoons: one can still read a sign which says CANTEEN, and a painted finger points to a sad edifice with broken roof and windows. A little further on there is a deep valley with little paths winding among the bushes and hillocks. Down there one cannot help noticing the wild flowers, and although the place is so near the town I have picked bunches of the fragrant, the pyramidal, and the spider orchis, and sometimes in thundery weather a bouquet of mixed flowers with several sorts of butterflies firmly attached, too drowsy to fly away.

WILLIAM PLOMER, *Electric Delights*

Brighton

Brighton is the receptacle of the fashion and off-scouring of London. The magnificence of the sea, and its, to use your own beautiful expression, 'everlasting voice', is drowned in the din and tumult of stage coaches, gigs, flys, etc., and the beach is only Piccadilly or worse by the seaside. Ladies dressed and undressed; gentlemen in morning-gowns and slippers, or without them or anything else, about knee deep in the breakers; footmen, children, nursery-maids, dogs, boys, fishermen, and Preventive Service men with hangers and pistols; rotten fish, and those hideous amphibious animals, the old bathing-women, whose language, both in oaths and voice, resembles men, all mixed together in endless and indecent confusion.

The genteeler part, or Marine Parade, is still more unnatural, with its trimmed and neat appearance, and the dandy jetty or Chain Pier, with its long and elegant strides into the sea a full quarter of a mile. . . . In short, there is nothing here for a painter but the breakers and the sky, which have been lovely indeed, and always varying.

JOHN CONSTABLE, letter to Dr Fisher, 1824

Dover Beach

The sea is calm tonight,
The tide is full, the moon lies fair
Upon the Straits; – on the French coast, the light
Gleams, and is gone; the cliffs of England stand,
Glimmering and vast, out in the tranquil bay.
Come to the window, sweet is the night air!
Only, from the long line of spray
Where the ebb meets the moon-blanch'd sand,
Listen! you hear the grating roar
Of pebbles which the waves suck back, and fling,
At their return, up the high strand,
Begin, and cease, and then again begin,
With tremulous cadence slow, and bring
The eternal note of sadness in.

MATTHEW ARNOLD

Most people who go on the West Pier at Brighton walk at once straight to the farthest part. This is the order and custom of pier promenading; you are to stalk along the deck till you reach the end, and there go round and round the band in a circle, like a horse tethered to an iron pin, or else sit down and admire those who do go round and round. No one looks back at the gradually extending beach and the fine curve of the shore. No one lingers where the surf breaks – immediately above it – listening to the remorseful sigh of the dying wave as it sobs back to the sea. There, looking downwards, the white edge of the surf recedes in hollow crescents, curve after curve for a mile or more, one succeeding before the first can disappear and be replaced by a fresh wave. A faint mistiness hangs above the beach at some distance, formed of the salt particles dashed into the air and suspended. At night, if the tide chances to be up, the white surf rushing in and returning immediately beneath has a strange effect, especially in its pitiless regularity. If one wave seems to break a little higher it is only in appearance, and because you have not watched long enough. In a certain number of times another will break there again; presently one will encroach the merest trifle; after a while another encroaches again, and the apparent irregularity is really sternly regular. The free wave has no liberty – it does not act for itself, – no real generous wildness. 'Thus far and no farther', is not a merciful saying. Cold and dread and pitiless, the wave claims its due – it stretches its arms to the fullest length, and does not pause or hearken to the desire of any human heart. Hopeless to appeal to is the unseen force that sends the white surge underneath to darken the pebbles to a certain line. The wetted pebbles are darker than the dry; even in the dusk they are easily distinguished. Something merciless is there not in this conjunction of restriction and impetus? Something outside human hope and thought – indifferent – cold?

Considering in this way, I wandered about fifty yards along the pier, and sat down in an abstracted way on the seat on the right side. Beneath, the clear green sea rolled in crestless waves towards the shore – they were moving 'without the animation of the wind', which had deserted them two days ago, and a hundred miles out at sea. Slower and slower, with an indolent undulation, rising and sinking of mere weight and devoid of impetus, the waves passed on, scarcely seeming to break the smoothness of the surface. At a little distance it seemed level; yet the boats every now and then sank deeply into the trough, and even a large fishing-smack rolled heavily. For it is the nature of a ground-swell to be exceedingly deceptive. Sometimes the waves are so far apart that the sea actually is level – smooth as the surface of a polished dining-table – till presently there appears a darker line slowly approaching, and a wave of considerable size comes in, advancing exactly like the crease in the cloth which the housemaid spreads on the table – the air rolling along underneath it forms a linen imitation of the ground-swell. These unexpected rollers are capital at upsetting boats just touching the beach; the boat is broadside on and the occupants in the water in a second. Today the ground-swell was more active, the waves closer together, not having had time to forget the force of the extinct gale. Yet the sea looked calm as a millpond – just the morning for a bath.

RICHARD JEFFERIES, *The Open Air*

To W.D.

This morning we had a row on the Sea. It is the height of holiday joy for a father to take his boys with him in a boat and row with them. No joy more sweet and pure than to see them get brown in the sun and grow stronger in the Sea air.

There are no dreams like 'Sea Dreams'. How grand it was last night after sunset to walk a quarter of a mile beyond our lodgings and find myself in a solitary white road with barley and wheat fields on each side, a hint of vast distance eastward, the Sea westward, the lighthouse with its steady white star, the lightship out at Sea with its red light going in and out, the first stars appearing, the soft fresh night breeze blowing, the hush, the calm, the sublime calm, 'the rising mind', the sense of God!

JAMES SMETHAM, *Letters*

CEREMONIES, RITUALS AND OCCASIONS

◆§ §◆

The English people love official processions, medieval costumes, wigs, lords, ermines, the antiquated gold royal coaches driving with King to Westminster for the Opening of Parliament, the heavy keys handed by the Lord Mayor to the King as he enters the City.

NIKOS KAZANTZAKIS, *England*

We are a country of ritualists, and we enjoy ceremony, Masonic functions, processions, taking the collection round, watching a fête being opened, and people being invested and, though we may sometimes laugh at them, we rather fancy the idea of being a Mayor or a Bishop or a Peer. And we do ceremonies with more dignity and reverence than any other nation. We complain a bit beforehand about what a bore it is going to be, all this dressing up, and then we dress up and produce something like the Coronation, which puts every other coronation in the world in the shade. Because we know how to deal with ceremony, we shine at agonizing public dinners. The putting on of best clothes, the oaths and searchings for lost studs beforehand, the washing behind the ears and round the neck, the clean collar etc., the getting there in time . . .

JOHN BETJEMAN, *The Compleat Imbiber*

The first view of the House did not strike me as so grand as the old House, but my mouth was stopped by '*Pro tempore* only, you know'. We went up an ignominiously small staircase, and the man at the bottom, piteously perspiring, cried out, 'On, on, ladies! don't stop the way! room enough above!' But there was one objection to going on, that there were no seats above: however, we made ourselves small – no great difficulty – and, taking to the wall, we left a scarcely practicable pass for those who, less wary and more obedient than ourselves, went up one by one to the highmost void. Fanny feared for me that I should never be able to *stand* it, when somehow or another my name was pronounced and heard by one of the Miss Southebys, who stretched her cordial hand. 'Glad – proud – glad – we'll squeeze – we'll make room for you between me and my friend Miss Fitzhugh'; and so I was bodkin, but never touched the bench till long after. I cast a lingering look at my deserted sisters twain. 'No, no, we can't do that!' so, that hope killed off, I took to make the best of my own selfish position, and surveyed all beneath me, from the black heads of the reporter gentlemen, with their pencils and papers before them in the form and desk immediately below me, to the depths of the hall, in all its long extent; and sprawling and stretching in the midst – with the feathered and lappeted and jewelled peeresses on their right, and their foreign excellencies on the left – were the long-robed, ermined judges, laying their wigs together and shaking hands, their wigs' many-curled tails shaking on their backs. And the wigs jointly and severally looked like so many vast white and gray birds'-nests from Brobdingnag, with a black hole at the top of each, for the birds to creep out or in. More and more scarlet-ermined dignitaries and nobles swarmed into the hall, and then, in at the scarlet door, came, with white ribbon shoulder-knots and streamers flying in all directions, a broad scarlet five-row-ermined figure, with high, bald forehead, facetious face, and jovial, hail-fellow-well-met countenance, princely withal, HRH the Duke of Cambridge, and the sidelong peeress benches stretched their fair hands, and he his ungloved royal hand hastily here and there and everywhere, and chattering so loud and long, that even the remote gallery could hear the 'Ha, ha, haw!' which followed ever and anon; and we blessed ourselves, and thought we should never hear the Queen; but I was told he would be silent when the Queen came, and so it proved.

The guns were heard: once, twice, and at the second all were silent: even His Royal Highness of Cambridge ceased to rustle and flutter, and stood nobly still.

Enter the crown and cushion and sword of state and mace –

the Queen, leaning on Prince Albert's arm. She did not go up the steps to the throne well – caught her foot and stumbled against the edge of the footstool, which was too high. She did not seat herself in a decided, queenlike manner, and after sitting down pottered too much with her drapery, arranging her petticoats. That footstool was much too high! her knees were crumpled up, and her figure, short enough already, was foreshortened as she sat, and her drapery did not come to the edge of the stool: as my neighbour Miss Fitzhugh whispered, 'Bad effect.' However and nevertheless, the better half of her looked perfectly ladylike and queenlike; her head finely shaped, and well held on her shoulders with her likeness of a kingly crown, that diadem of diamonds. Beautifully fair the neck and arms; and the arms moved gracefully, and never too much. I could not at that distance judge of her countenance, but I heard people on the bench near me saying that she looked 'divinely gracious'.

Dead silence: more of majesty implied in that silence than in all the magnificence around. She spoke, low and well: 'My lords and gentlemen, be seated.' Then she received from the lord-in-waiting her speech, and read: her voice, perfectly distinct and clear, was heard by us ultimate auditors; it was not quite so fine a voice as I had been taught to expect; it had not the full rich tones nor the varied powers and inflections of a perfect voice. She read with good sense, as if she perfectly understood, but did not fully or warmly feel, what she was reading. It was more a girl's well-read lesson than a Queen pronouncing her speech. She did not lay emphasis sufficient to mark the gradations of importance in the subjects, and she did not make pauses enough. The best-pronounced paragraphs were those about France and Ireland, her firm determination to preserve inviolate the legislative union; and 'I am resolved to act in strict conformity with this declaration' she pronounced strongly and well. She showed less confidence in reading about the suspension of the elective franchise, and in the conclusion, emphasis and soul were wanting, when they were called for, when she said, 'In full confidence of your loyalty and wisdom, and with an earnest prayer to Almighty GOD,' etc.

Her Majesty's exit I was much pleased to look at, it was so graceful and so gracious. She took time enough for all her motions, noticing all properly, from 'my dear uncle' – words I distinctly heard as she passed the Duke of Cambridge – to the last expectant fair one at the doorway. The Queen vanished: buzz, noise, the clatter rose, and all were in commotion, and the tide of scarlet and ermine flowed and ebbed; and after an immense time the throngs of people bonneted and shawled, came forth from all the side niches and windows, and down from the upper galleries, and then places unknown gave up their occupants, and all the outward halls were filled with the living mass. . . .

MARIA EDGEWORTH, *Life and Letters*

The House of Commons

The members sat with their hats on, but the Speaker was uncovered, if a man can be said to be uncovered who is buried in tow. They sit on benches with backs of the ordinary height, and I counted six members with one foot on the backs of the benches before them, and three with both feet. The latter were very interesting attitudes, a good deal resembling those which your country buck is apt to take in an American bar-room, and which I have seen in a church. I do not mention these trifles to draw any great moral or political consequences from them, but simply because similar things have been commented on in connexion with Congress, and ascribed to democracy. I am of opinion political systems have little to do with these *tours de force*, but that there is rather a tendency in the Anglo-Saxon race to put the heels higher than the head.

Behind the Speaker's chair two members were stretched at full length, asleep. I presume the benches they occupied were softer than common, for two or three others seemed anxiously watching the blissful moment of their waking, with an evident intention to succeed them. One did arise, and a successor was in his place in less than a minute. That I may dispose of this part of the subject, once for all, I will add that, during the evening, three young men came into the side gallery within fifteen feet of me, and stretched themselves on the benches, where they were not visible to those in the body of the house. Two were disposed to sleep, rationally, but one of them kept pulling their coats and legs in a way to render it no easy matter, when all three retired together laughing, as if it were a bad job. I should think neither of the three was five-and-twenty. . . .

As respects the cries, so much spoken of, some of them are droll enough. Of the 'Hear, hear, hear' I shall say nothing, unless it be to tell you that they are so modulated as to express different emotions. There is a member or two, just now, that are rather expert in crowing like a cock, and I have known an attempt to bleat like a lamb, but I think it was a failure.

I was quite unprepared for one species of interruption, which is a new invention, and seems likely to carry all before it, for a time. Something that was said excited a most pronounced dissatisfaction among the whigs, and they set up a noise that was laughably like the qua-a-cking of a flock of ducks. For some time I did not know what to make of it – then I thought the cry was 'Bar, bar, bar' and fancied that they wished a delinquent to be put at their bar; but I believe, after all, it was no more than the introduction of the common French interjection 'bah!' which signifies dissent. The word is so sonorous, that

189

twenty or thirty men can make a very pretty uproar by a diligent use of it.

You will ask what the Speaker says to these interruptions? He says, *'Order*, ORDER,' – and there the matter ends. I shall say nothing against these practices, for I do not believe they essentially affect the interests of the country, and, as Fuseli used to tell his wife, when she got in a pet – *'Schwear*, my dear – do; *schwear* a little, it will do you good,' – it may be a relief to a man to break out occasionally in these vocal expressions of feeling, especially to those who cannot, very conveniently to themselves, say anything else.

JAMES FENIMORE COOPER, England

The Members file in to the chamber of the House of Commons, take a pinch of snuff if they want it from the coffin-like box in which the doorkeeper sits. They bow to the Chair – yet not to the Chair. There was an altar there in old days, and (probably without knowing it) they are bowing to the altar. Never if we can help it do we forget the past in the present. The present chamber replaces the one destroyed in the war and has that lack of distinction that London has often drifted into; to be distinguished is an accomplishment that has been lost by a generation which pursues the commonplace with something amounting to pedantry. The present chamber might be an out-of-date municipal library.

Still the never-never land of the Victorian Gothic imagination survives. One is assaulted by two sensations, the religious and the historical, in the light of which the Victorians conducted the business of the most advanced industrial society of the world for three-quarters of a century. Here the police are at their most melting and considerate, the ushers tall and statesmanlike in their black. The House is one of those places where London unmistakably does 'the thing' well and with that briskness which the public institution always brings out in our torpid souls, the touch and performance are light and clever.The actors know their parts. The public crowd who wait for the Speaker's Procession which passes every day through the light Central Hall have a homely and ludicrous look in this gay Gothic setting; for the defect of a Gothic background is that it makes twentieth-century man and woman look vulgar and pathetic. The scene may have been more tolerable in the Victorian age, when clothes were severer, or more elaborate than they are now; but even then one must have felt the human inadequacy in these surroundings – a matter Mark Twain and the English humorists felt hilariously about the whole Gothic infatuation. But when, suddenly, a loud voice calls out 'The Speaker', and another voice calls out sharply 'Hats off', there is a silence in which one realizes that what is about to happen is not a joke at all. One is going to see the ghosts walk. One hears their rapid step. They go by in their black with the briskness of a dream and give a cold thrill for a second or two to the blood. Exactly at half past two, in perfect step, expressionless, chins a little raised, as if on some duty, exalted and exquisitely unnecessary, five men go by, dressed in black: the Sergeant-at-Arms; the mace-bearer, holding the mace before him; the wigged Speaker himself, in black silk knee-breeches and buckled shoes; his train-bearer, holding up his short robe; and his chaplain bringing up the rear. A stir of air follows them. They have vanished. The strange moment, with no clowning in it, is eerie; it is one of London's brilliant little set pieces. In twenty seconds the 'thing' has been 'done'.

V. S. PRITCHETT, *London Perceived*

Churchill's Lying in State

It was the last week of January 1965. Churchill's funeral took place on Saturday 30 January. The Lying in State lasted throughout the previous fortnight. The queue, starting from the gates of the House of Commons, curled round over Westminster Bridge, then along Lambeth Palace Road, thence over Lambeth Bridge to Millbank leading to Westminster Hall in which the catafalque was placed. I understood that it meant about four hours in the queue before reaching the Hall. It flowed on throughout every day and every night.

It occurred to me that this was one of those historic occasions in which it would be good to participate. I was living in Ewell in Surrey at the time, and I thought that if I drove up on the Tuesday of the second week in the middle of the night, arriving at about 3 a.m., the queue would surely be short, and I wouldn't have to join it for more than an hour before reaching the cata-falque. So I went up and parked my car in the vicinity of Parliament Square – for no policeman was making the slightest objection as to where one put a car on this occasion.

I hastened to walk across the Square and was pleased to find no queue in sight. Then in high spirits I walked quickly over Westminster Bridge, and turned to the right into Lambeth Palace Road – to be confronted almost at once by an enormously wide queue, a long distance from the bridge. My heart sank. It is an eccentricity of mine to do things on impulse without taking simple precautions. It was a cold night, and I was wearing only a light overcoat and thin socks, and absolutely the wrong kind of shoes. By the time I had reached Lambeth Bridge, I had become alarmed by my predicament, but hoped that I would make it.

I looked round at this great queue of people, so long and wide. Many were young and must have been children during the war, perhaps not yet born at its outset. Many others were middle-aged – they had heard that voice coming to them over the wireless, whether to groups or into lonely rooms. Twenty years had passed since the final triumph of this man. But neither the young nor the middle-aged were thinking of those last years, but of what he had been, of what he was in their imagination. He was the man who had overcome Hitler. He had promised nothing. He did not rant. He never smiled. There was melancholy in his cadence, and there was understanding of simple people when he spoke of 'that bad man over there'. Now his body was soon to disappear from the surface of the earth.

I spoke to nobody, and I heard no memorable remark. It had become very cold. I welcomed this. It was far more appropriate for the sombre scene than a warm summer night would have been. But on account of my faulty clothing I became anxious. Something must be done. After we had at last crossed Lambeth Bridge, the queue took an enormous loop around a Green before joining Millbank. In the middle of this Green a marquee had been erected to serve the purposes of a lavatory. I had a hat on and it occurred to me that if I stepped out of my place in the queue, entered the tent, and then emerged hatless from it, I could join the far end of the loop without attracting any notice. And indeed I did accomplish this quite easily.

This reprehensible tactic cut out at least an hour of my queue-crawling, yet it was not until 6.30 a.m. that I was able to mount the steps of Westminster Hall and go inside. What a change! I came into wonderful warm air and a cathedral peace. A long staircase led down to the floor of the great hall in which the catafalque stood. Our queue, the river of people come to pay homage to Churchill, flowed slowly down this long staircase. We were not chivvied by any policemen, there was no 'keep moving, please', all was discreet courtesy. In fact I paused on my way down and stood still to watch something. There were four sentinels stationed at the catafalque, one at each corner. They were relieved at regular intervals by fresh guards. It was my good fortune while descending the stairs to see a relief party in action.

From a door on the left side of the catafalque, and higher up, four sentinels appeared. The other four standing by the coffin had their rifles in the 'at ease' position, their legs apart, their heads bowed. They were motionless as any statue. Gradually the four men from above, in obedience to no verbal command, with incomparable grace of movement, each soundlessly approached the separate sentinels, and stood behind them. Then quietly the statues came to life; their limbs assumed slow motion; their bowed heads were raised: silently they came to attention and sloped arms, and each with the same rhythm left the catafalque by the way the others had come – who now slowly ordered arms, stood at ease, bowed their heads, until their figures too were frozen.

After passing the catafalque I stopped before the exit to look back at the steady stream of people descending the stairs. That stream had flowed during all the previous week, night and day, and would continue day and night until the ending of this second week.

As I left the Hall I stumbled and fell to the ground. Two policemen quietly restored me to the perpendicular. This indignity did not bother me at all. I had seen something I would not forget. After seventeen years I put it in words now as if, for me, it had been yesterday. There was a message too, could I but read it, as to the meaning of Homage and of Leadership.

JOHN STEWART COLLIS, *Spectator*, 10 January 1982

Here, as in other courts of justice in London, the judges sit in blue-black togas, which are trimmed with light-blue violet, and wear white powdered wigs, with which black eyes and whiskers frequently contrast in the drollest manner. They sit around a long green table on high chairs at the upper end of the hall, just where a Scripture text, warning against unjust judgments, is placed before their eyes. On either side are benches for the jurymen, and places where the prosecutors and witnesses stand. Directly opposite the judges is the place for the accused, which latter do not sit on 'the poor sinners' bench', as in the criminal courts of France and Rhenish Germany, but must stand upright behind a singular plank, which is carved above like a narrow arched gate. In this an optic mirror is placed, by means of which the judge is enabled to accurately observe the countenance of the accused. Before the latter certain green leaves or herbs are placed to strengthen their nerves – and it may be that this is sometimes necessary, when a man is in danger of losing his life. On the judges' table I saw similar green leaves, and even a rose. I know not why it was, but the sight of that rose affected me strangely. A red blooming rose, the flower of love and of spring, upon the terrible judges' table of the Old Bailey! It was close, gloomy, and sultry in the hall. Everything seemed so fearfully vexatious, so insanely serious! The people present looked as though spiders were creeping over their shy and fearful faces.

HEINRICH HEINE, *English Fragments*

Exeter, March '92. The Cathedral bells are ringing merrily all today. I ask the reason, and find it is to celebrate the coming of the Judges.

GEORGE GISSING, Commonplace Book

Wed. 23 March 1768. I had this morning been at Tyburn seeing the execution of Mr Gibson, the attorney, for forgery, and of Benjamin Payne for highway robbery. It is a curious turn, but I never can resist seeing executions . . . I was on a scaffold close by. Payne was a poor young man of nineteen. He was pale as death, and half a corpse before the rope was put round his neck. Mr Gibson came in a coach with some of his friends, and I declare I cannot conceive a more perfect calmness and manly resolution than his behaviour. He was dressed in a full suit of black, wore his own hair cut round and a hat, was a man about fifty, and as he drove along it was impossible to perceive the least sign of dejection or gloom about him. He was helped up on the cart. The rope was put round his neck, and he stood with the most perfect composure, ate a sweet orange, and seemed rationally devout during prayers by Mr Moore, the ordinary of Newgate, who is really a good man and most earnest in the duties of his sad office, which I think a very important one.

JAMES BOSWELL

1805

At Viscount Nelson's lavish funeral,
    While the mob milled and yelled about St Paul's,
A General chatted with an Admiral:

'One of your Colleagues, Sir, remarked today
    That Nelson's *exit*, though to be lamented,
Falls not inopportunely, in its way.'

'He was a thorn in our flesh,' came the reply –
    'The most bird-witted, unaccountable,
Odd little runt that ever I did spy.

'One arm, one peeper, vain as Pretty Poll,
   A meddler, too, in foreign politics
And gave his heart in pawn to a plain moll.

'He would dare lecture us Sea Lords, and then
   Would treat his ratings as though men of honour
And play at leap-frog with his midshipmen!

'We tried to box him down, but up he popped,
   And when he'd banged Napoleon at the Nile
Became too much the hero to be dropped.

'You've heard that Copenhagen "blind eye" story?
   We'd tied him to Nurse Parker's apron-strings –
By G—d, he snipped them through and snatched the glory!'

'Yet,' cried the General, 'six-and-twenty sail
   Captured and sunk by him off Tráfalgár –
That writes a handsome *finis* to the tale.'

'Handsome enough. The seas are England's now.
   That fellow's foibles need no longer plague us.
He died most creditably, I'll allow.'

'And, Sir, the secret of his victories?'
   'By his unServicelike, familiar ways, Sir,
He made the whole Fleet love him, damn his eyes!'

ROBERT GRAVES

A Funeral, 1853

In the afternoon, at three o'clock, I attended the funeral of Captain Auld. Being ushered into the dining-room of his boarding-house, I found brandy, gin, and wine set out on a tray, together with some little spice-cakes. By-and-by came in a woman, who asked if I were going to the funeral; and then proceeded to put a mourning band on my hat. After waiting the better part of an hour, nobody else appeared, although several shipmasters had promised to attend. Hereupon the undertaker was anxious to set forth; but the landlady, who was arrayed in shining black

196

silk, thought it a shame that the poor man should be buried with such small attendance. So we waited a little longer, during which interval I heard the landlady's daughter sobbing and wailing in the entry; and but for this tender-heartedness there would have been no tears at all. Finally we set forth, – the undertaker, a friend of his, and a young man, perhaps the landlady's son, and myself, in the black-plumed coach, and the landlady, her daughter, and a female friend, in the coach behind. Previous to this, however, everybody had taken some wine or spirits; for it seemed to be considered disrespectful not to do so.

Before us went the plumed hearse, a stately affair, with a bas-relief of funereal figures upon its sides. We proceeded quite across the city to the Necropolis, where the coffin was carried into a chapel, in which we found already another coffin, and another set of mourners, awaiting the clergyman. Anon he appeared, – a stern, broad-framed, large, and bald-headed man, in a black-silk gown. He mounted his desk, and read the service in quite a feeble and unimpressive way, though with no lack of solemnity. This done, our four bearers took up the coffin, and carried it out of the chapel; but descending the steps, and, perhaps, having taken a little too much brandy, one of them stumbled, and down came the coffin – not quite to the ground, however; for they grappled with it, and contrived, with a great struggle, to prevent the misadventure. But I really expected to see poor Captain Auld burst forth among us in his grave-clothes.

The Necropolis is quite a handsome burial-place, shut in by high walls, so overrun with shrubbery that no part of the brick or stone is visible. Part of the space within is an ornamental garden, with flowers and green turf; the rest is strewn with flat gravestones, and a few raised monuments; and straight avenues run to and fro between. Captain Auld's grave was dug nine feet deep. It is his own for twelve months; but, if his friends do not choose to give him a stone, it will become a common grave at the end of that time; and four or five more bodies may then be piled upon his. Every one seemed greatly to admire the grave; the undertaker praised it, and also the dry-ness of its site, which he took credit to himself for having chosen. The grave-digger, too, was very proud of its depth, and the neatness of his handiwork. The clergyman, who had marched in advance of us from the chapel, now took his stand at the head of the grave, and, lifting his hat, proceeded with what remained of the service, while we stood bareheaded around. When he came to a particular part, 'ashes to ashes, dust to dust', the undertaker lifted a handful of earth, and threw it rattling on the coffin, – so did the landlady's son, and so did I. After the funeral, the undertaker's friend, an elderly, coarse-looking man, looked round him, and remarked that 'the grass had never grown on the parties who died in the cholera year'; but at this the undertaker laughed in scorn.

As we returned to the gate of the cemetery, the sexton met us, and pointed to a small office, on entering which we found the clergyman, who was waiting for his burial-fees. There was now a dispute between the clergyman and the undertaker; the former wishing to receive the whole amount for the grave-stone, which the undertaker, of course, refused to pay. I explained how the matter stood; on which the clergyman acquiesced, civilly enough; but it was very strange to see the worldly, business-like way in which he entered into this squabble, so soon after burying poor Captain Auld.

During our drive back in the mourning-coach, the under-taker, his friend, and the landlady's son still kept descanting on the excellence of the grave – 'Such a fine grave' – 'Such a nice grave' – 'Such a splendid grave' – and, really, they seemed almost to think it worth while to die, for the sake of being buried there. They deemed it an especial pity that such a grave should ever become a common grave. 'Why,' said they to me, 'by paying the extra price you may have it for your own grave, or for your family!' meaning that we should have a right to pile ourselves over the defunct Captain. I wonder how the English ever attain to any conception of a future existence, since they so overburden themselves with earth and mortality in their ideas of funerals. A drive with an undertaker, in a sable-plumed coach! – talking about graves! – and yet he was a jolly old fellow, wonderfully corpulent, with a smile breaking out easily all over his face, – although, once in a while, he looked professionally lugubrious.

All the time the scent of that horrible mourning-coach is in my nostrils, and I breathe nothing but a funeral atmosphere.

NATHANIEL HAWTHORNE, *English Notebooks*

The moment the noise ceases, up starts the toastmaster – 'Gentlemen, charge your glasses, if you please!' Decanters having been handed about, and glasses filled, the toastmaster proceeds in a regular ascending scale: 'Gentlemen – *air* – you – all – charged? Pray – silence – gentlemen – for – the cha-i-r.' The chairman rises, and after stating that he feels it quite unnecessary to preface the toast he is about to propose, with any observations whatever, wanders into a maze of sentences, and flounders about in the most extraordinary manner, presenting a lamentable spectacle of mystified humanity, until he arrives at the words 'constitutional sovereign of these realms', at which elderly gentlemen exclaim 'Bravo!' and hammer the table tremendously with their knife-handles. 'Under any circumstances, it would give him the greatest pride, it would give him the greatest pleasure – he might almost say, it would afford him satisfaction (cheers) to propose that toast. What must be his feelings, then, when he has the gratification of announcing, that he has received her Majesty's commands to apply to the Treasurer of her Majesty's Household, for her Majesty's annual donation of 25*l.* in aid of the funds of this charity!' This announcement (which has been regularly made by every chairman, since the first foundation of the charity, forty-two years ago) calls forth the most vociferous applause; the toast is drunk with a great deal of cheering and knocking; and 'God save the Queen' is sung by the 'professional gentlemen'; the unprofessional gentlemen joining in the chorus, and giving the national anthem an effect which the newspapers, with great justice, describe as 'perfectly electrical' . . .

After a short interval, occupied in singing and toasting, the secretary puts on his spectacles, and proceeds to read the report and list of subscriptions, the latter being listened to with great attention. 'Mr Smith, one guinea – Mr Tompkins, one guinea – Mr Wilson, one guinea – Mr Hickson, one guinea – Mr Nixon, one guinea – Mr Charles Nixon, one guinea – (hear, hear!) – Mr James Nixon, one guinea – Mr Thomas Nixon, one pound one (tremendous applause). Lord Fitz Binkle, the chairman of the day, in addition to an annual donation of fifteen pounds – thirty guineas (prolonged knocking: several gentlemen knock the stems off their wine-glasses, in the vehemence of their

approbation). Lady Fitz Binkle, in addition to an annual donation of ten pound – twenty pound' (protracted knocking and
shouts of 'Bravo!'). The list being at length concluded, the
chairman rises, and proposes the health of the secretary, than
whom he knows no more zealous or estimable individual. The
secretary, in returning thanks, observes that *he* knows no more
excellent individual than the chairman – except the senior
officer of the charity, whose health *he* begs to propose. The
senior officer, in returning thanks, observes that *he* knows no
more worthy man than the secretary – except Mr Walker, the
auditor, whose health *he* begs to propose. Mr Walker, in returning thanks, discovers some other estimable individual, to
whom alone the senior officer is inferior – and so they go on
toasting and lauding and thanking: the only other toast of
importance being 'The Lady Patronesses now present!', on
which all the gentlemen turn their faces towards the ladies'
gallery, shouting tremendously; and little priggish men, who
have imbibed more wine than usual, kiss their hands and
exhibit distressing contortions of visage.

CHARLES DICKENS, *Sketches by Boz*

Oh shall I ever forget the sight of the only City dinner I ever
attended in my life: at the hall of the Right Worshipful Company of Chimney-Sweepers – it was in May, and a remarkable
pea-season. The hall was decorated with banners and escutch-
eons of deceased *chummies* – martial music resounded from the
balconies as the Master of the Company and the great ones
marched in. We sat down, grace was said, the tureen-covers
removed, and instantly a silence in the hall – a breathless
silence – and then a great gurgle! – grwlwlwlw it sounded like.
The Worshipful Company were sucking in the turtle.

WILLIAM MAKEPEACE THACKERAY

The Royal Literary Fund Dinner, 1858

The dinner was rather bad, like all public dinners. Champagne
came with the roast chicken, and the toastmaster, who stood
behind Palmerston's chair, proposed the health of the Queen.

All rose from their seats and nine ear-splitting 'hurrahs' – three times three – resounded through the hall. The toastmaster was the first to cheer and gave the signal for the rest with a rolled-up scroll of paper which he held in his hand like a wand. The health of the queen was drunk with great enthusiasm; she is very popular with her subjects, and, besides, as an English friend of mine remarked, every Englishman who drinks the health of his queen also drinks his own health, so how is one not to be enthusiastic? The shouts, accompanied by the banging of knives on the table, died down and were at once renewed. Palmerston then got up and began his speech. . . . What interested me especially was Palmerston's diction. He spoke rather slowly, as though hesitating, searched for words, and in between finding them kept on saying, 'er – er', accompanying his speech by movements of the right hand, and always found a beautiful and precise ending for his sentences. This clumsiness, this continuous use of 'er', these stutterings, are a characteristic feature of English speech; people like Palmerston, who are always making public speeches at meetings, in Parliament and at dinners, never get rid of it. I was told by Englishmen that Fox, Pitt and Sheridan spoke like that; and, strange to say, this characteristic becomes intelligible and almost pleasant as soon as you get to know the character of the English; it adds a sort of naturalness to their speech, a touch of good humour and improvisation.

IVAN TURGENEV

The Charity Children at St Paul's

I was in London at the beginning of June when a cutting from a newspaper falling into my hands by chance, I saw that the *Anniversary Meeting of the Charity Children* was to take place at St Paul's Cathedral. I at once set out to get a ticket, and after writing several letters and taking different steps I at last obtained one by the kindness of Mr Goss, the organist of the Cathedral.

By ten o'clock the approaches to St Paul's were crowded with people, and I had some trouble in getting through. When I got to the organ loft reserved for the choir, composed of men and boys to the number of seventy, I was given a copy of a bass part which they asked me to sing with the rest, also a surplice which

I had to put on, so that my black coat should not clash with the white costumes of the rest of the choir. Disguised thus as a cleric, I awaited the performance with a sort of vague emotion, roused by the spectacle. Nine almost vertical amphitheatres, sixteen tiers high, had been put up for the children, under the dome and in the choir in front of the organ. The six under the dome formed a sort of hexagonal circus opening only East and West. From the latter opening stretched an inclined plane ending above the main entrance; it was already covered by a huge congregation, who were able in this way to see and hear everything perfectly even from the furthest seats. To the left of the gallery where we were, in front of the organ, there was a stand for seven or eight trumpets and drummers. On this stand a large mirror was placed so that the musicians might see the reflection of the choir-master beating time in the distance, in an angle under the dome; whence he controlled the whole of the massed choirs. This mirror also acted as a guide to the organist whose back was turned to the choir. Banners planted all round the vast amphitheatre – the sixteenth tier reached almost to the capitals of the columns – marked the place of each school, and bore the names of the parishes and districts of London to which they belonged. As the children came in and filled the amphitheatre from top to bottom, the sight reminded me of the phenomenon of crystallization under a microscope. This crystal compound of human particles was of two colours, the dark blue of the boys on the top tiers, and the white of the girls on the lower. Further as the boys had brass plates or silver medals on their jackets, these glittered as they moved like a thousand intermittent sparks on the dark background. The appearance of the girls' seats was still more curious; the green and pink ribbons worn by these little white maids, made this part of the amphitheatre look exactly like a snow-covered mountain with blades of grass and flowers peeping out here and there. Then there were the different hues among the congregation, the crimson throne of the Archbishop of Canterbury, the richly decorated benches of the Lord Mayor and the aristocracy, and high up at the other end the gilded pipes of the great organ; imagine this magnificent church of St Paul's, the largest in the World after St Peter's, framing the whole scene, and you will still have only a very faint sketch of this incomparable sight. The magical effect was enhanced by the order, the quietude and the serenity which reigned everywhere. No stage setting however admirable can ever approach the reality which even now appears to me like a dream. As the children, in their new clothes came to their seats with happy serious faces, without noise but with a certain pride, I heard my English friends saying to each other: 'What a scene! What a scene! . . .' and I was deeply stirred when, the *six thousand five hundred* little singers being seated, the ceremony began.

After a chord on the organ, there burst forth in gigantic unison the first hymn sung by this unique choir:

> All people that on earth do dwell
> Sing to the Lord with cheerful voice.

It is useless to try and give you an idea of such a musical effect. It compares with the power and beauty of the finest vocal masses you have ever heard, just as St Paul's compares with a village church. I may add that this hymn, with its broad notes and sublime style, is supported by superb harmonies which the organ gives out without drowning it. I was agreeably surprised to hear that the music of this hymn, for a long time attributed to Luther, is by Claude Goudimel, choir-master at Lyons in the *XVI* Century.

Though I was trembling and felt a sense of oppression, I held up, and managed to control myself well enough to be able to take part in the psalms which were next chanted by the professional choir. Boyce's *Te Deum* (written in 1760), a piece without character, calmed me down.

With the Coronation Anthem in which the children joined the small professional choir from time to time, with solemn exclamations such as: *God Save the King! – Long live the King! – May the King live for ever! – Amen! Hallelujah!* I began again to be electrified. I stopped several times, in spite of my neighbour, who kept on pointing to the bar we had got to in his part, thinking that I had lost my place. But when I heard the psalms in three time by J. Ganthony, an old English master (1774), sung by all the voices, with trumpets, drums and the organ – a truly inspired composition with its grand harmonies, my feelings overcame me, and I had to use my Music as Agamemnon did his toga, to hide my face. After this during the sermon preached by the Archbishop of Canterbury one of the ushers took me round – I was still *lacrymans* – to different parts of the church, to see the spectacle in all its aspects. He left me among the smart people near the pulpit, as it were at the base of the crater of the vocal volcano. And when the eruption began again, for the last psalm, I must admit that the effect was twice as great there as elsewhere. As I went out, I met old Cramer, who in his excitement, forgetting his perfect command of French, began calling out to me in Italian: *Cosa stupenda! stupenda! La gloria dell'Inghilterra!*

HECTOR BERLIOZ, *Memoirs*

Family Prayers

Today, 27th May 1835, I lunched at Lord Radnor's house. Before coming to table Lord Radnor went to his study; Lady Radnor and his daughters went there too; after a moment eleven or twelve women- and eight or ten men-servants came in. They walked in formal order of hierarchic precedence, as was easily seen by the age and dress of each of them. At the head of the women was the children's governess; then the housekeeper and the chambermaid and then the lower servants. The steward came at the head of the men and the grooms at the tail. These twenty people took their places round the room and knelt down looking towards the wall. Near the fireplace, Lord and Lady Radnor and Lady Louisa knelt down too, and Lord Radnor read a prayer aloud, the servants giving the responses. This sort of little service lasted six or eight minutes, after which the male and female servants got up and went out in the same order to resume their work.

ALEXIS DE TOCQUEVILLE, *Journey to England*

Queen Victoria's Jubilee

22 June 1897. In afternoon of Jubilee procession.
Edward Burne-Jones: It was all surprisingly successful – but all the boasting of the papers is so dreadful; it makes one wonder

that a thunderbolt doesn't fall upon London. They're so silly as not to know that the gods do not love.

I: *What?*

E B-J: The pride of cockiness. And all this enthusiasm spent over one little unimportant old lady in the one effort of imagination of the English race. It's curious, but rather pretty. There was one set of men near where we were, that won great favour. It was a regiment that kept the ground in front of Downing Street – the Seaforth Highlanders. They were in the highest good humour with everybody, and the pipers puffed away and kept walking backwards and forwards swelling with such pride and excitement that their naked calves seemed to turn upwards – making such a beastly row that I loathe and detest above all others – till I nearly went mad – for as you know the noise of Scotch bagpipes is the one sound I can't bear. Such savage, barbarous people they looked. Excellent people no doubt and in the best of tempers they were, but in that dress with tight plaid trousers and huge headdress of ostrich feathers they looked like South Sea Islanders altogether. There was an old boy on horseback who kept riding up and down and screaming at them and you could see his ridiculous bottom as he sat on his saddle. And he had brass-coloured eyebrows and moustaches and a pink face. Literally brass-coloured his hair was. He was a sight! It is said she (the poor old Queen) was very pleased with it all and wanted to go and see the illuminations, but Radford wouldn't let her.

I: Fancy the Queen of London to be under the command of her head policeman!

E B-J: Oh, he wouldn't hear of it – wasn't it rather a shame. There was a great German in the procession with an eagle on his helmet.

I: A white one?

E B-J: No, it was a metal one and I instantly hated him. He was a louring looking devil. He was such an overbearing huge ironmade wretch that the few moments' sight of him put me in a fury. (*Organ in the street.*) Ah, that feels as though life were beginning to take its old place, the organs beginning again in the street; now we can go to work quietly once more – once in a lifetime's enough for a Jubilee.

Burne-Jones Talking

Going Back to School

The other evening, at about seven o'clock, I was in a swift hansom. My hat was tilted at a gay angle, and, for all I was muffled closely, my gloves betokened a ceremonious attire. I was smoking *la cigarette d'appetit*, and was quite happy. Outside Victoria my cab was stopped by a file of other cabs, that were following one another in at the main entrance of the station. I noticed, on one of them, a small hat-box, a newish trunk and a corded play-box, and I caught one glimpse of a very small, pale boy in a billicock-hat. He was looking at me through the side-window. If Envy was ever inscribed on any face, it was inscribed on the face of that very small, pale boy. 'There,' I murmured, 'but for the grace of God, goes Max Beerbohm!'

My first thought, then, was for myself. I could not but plume me on the contrast of my own state with his. But, gradually, I became fulfilled with a very great compassion for him. I understood the boy's Envy so well. It was always the most bitter thing, in my own drive to the station, to see other people, quite happy, as it seemed, with no upheaval of their lives; people in cabs, who were going out to dinner and would sleep in London; grown-up people! Than the impotent despair of those drives – I had exactly fifteen of them – I hope that I shall never experience a more awful emotion. Those drives have something, surely, akin with drowning. In their course the whole of a boy's home-life passes before his eyes, every phase of it standing out against the black curtain of his future. The author of *Vice-Versa* has well analyzed the feeling, and he is right, I think, in saying that all boys, of whatsoever temperament, are preys to it. Well do I remember how, on the last day of the holidays, I used always to rise early, and think that I had got twelve more whole hours of happiness, and how those hours used to pass me with mercifully slow feet. . . . Three more hours! . . . Sixty more minutes! . . . Five! . . . I used to draw upon my tips for a first-class ticket, that I might not be plunged suddenly among my companions, with their hectic and hollow mirth, their dreary disinterment of last term's jokes. I used to revel in the thought that there were many stations before G——. . . The dreary walk, with my small bag, up the hill! I was not one of those who made a rush for the few cabs . . . The awful geniality of the House Master! The jugs in the dormitory! . . . Next morning, the bell that woke me! The awakening!

MAX BEERBOHM, *More*

RELIGION

Church Going

Once I am sure there's nothing going on
I step inside, letting the door thud shut.
Another church: matting, seats, and stone,
And little books; sprawlings of flowers, cut
For Sunday, brownish now; some brass and stuff
Up at the holy end; the small neat organ;
And a tense, musty, unignorable silence,
Brewed God knows how long. Hatless, I take off
My cycle-clips in awkward reverence,

Move forward, run my hand around the font.
From where I stand, the roof looks almost new –
Cleaned, or restored? Someone would know: I don't.
Mounting the lectern, I peruse a few
Hectoring large-scale verses, and pronounce
'Here endeth' much more loudly than I'd meant.
The echoes snigger briefly. Back at the door
I sign the book, donate an Irish sixpence,
Reflect the place was not worth stopping for.

Yet stop I did: in fact I often do,
And always end much at a loss like this,
Wondering what to look for; wondering, too,
When churches fall completely out of use
What we shall turn them into, if we shall keep
A few cathedrals chronically on show,
Their parchment, plate and pyx in locked cases,
And let the rest rent-free to rain and sheep.
Shall we avoid them as unlucky places?

Or, after dark, will dubious women come
To make their children touch a particular stone;
Pick simples for a cancer; or on some
Advised night see walking a dead one?
Power of some sort or other will go on
In games, in riddles, seemingly at random;
But superstition, like belief, must die,
And what remains when disbelief has gone?
Grass, weedy pavement, brambles, buttress, sky.

A shape less recognizable each week,
A purpose more obscure. I wonder who
Will be the last, the very last, to seek
This place for what it was; one of the crew
That tap and jot and know what rood-lofts were?
Some ruin-bibber, randy for antique,
Or Christmas-addict, counting on a whiff
Of gown-and-bands and organ-pipes and myrrh?
Or will he be my representative,

Bored, uninformed, knowing the ghostly silt
Dispersed, yet tending to this cross of ground
Through suburb scrub because it held unspilt
So long and equably what since is found
Only in separation – marriage, and birth,
And death, and thoughts of these – for which was built
This special shell? For, though I've no idea
What this accoutred frowsty barn is worth,
It pleases me to stand in silence here;

A serious house on serious earth it is,
In whose blent air all our compulsions meet,
Are recognized, and robed as destinies.
And that much never can be obsolete,
Since someone will forever be surprising
A hunger in himself to be more serious,
And gravitating with it to this ground,
Which, he once heard, was proper to grow wise in,
If only that so many dead lie round.

PHILIP LARKIN

England is almost the only country in the world (even at present) where there is not some favourite religious spot, where absurd lies, little bits of cloth, feathers, rusty nails, splinters and other invaluable relics, are treasured up, and in defence of which the whole population are willing to turn out and perish as one man.

SYDNEY SMITH, *Edinburgh Review*, 1824

I will not shrink from uttering my firm conviction that it would be a gain to this country, were it bigoted, more gloomy, more fierce in its religion than at present it shows itself to be. Not, of course, that I think the tempers of mind herein implied desirable, which would be an evident absurdity; but I think them infinitely more desirable and more promising than a heathen obduracy, and a cold, self-sufficient, self-wise tranquillity.

J. H. NEWMAN, *Parochial and Plain Sermons*

The English Cathedral

And now I wish that the reader ... would imagine himself for a little time in a quiet English cathedral town, and walk with me to the west front of its cathedral. Let us go together up the more retired street, at the end of which we can see the pinnacles of one of the towers, and then through the low grey gateway, with its battlemented top and small latticed window in the centre, into the inner private-looking road or close, where nothing goes in but the carts of the tradesmen who supply the bishop and the chapter, and where there are little shaven grass-plots, fenced in by neat rails, before old-fashioned groups of somewhat diminutive and excessively trim houses, with little oriel and bay windows jutting out here and there, and deep wooden cornices and eaves painted cream colour and white, and small porches to their doors in the shape of cockle-shells, or little, crooked, thick, indescribable wooden gables warped a little on one side; and so forward till we come to larger houses, also old-fashioned, but of red brick, and with gardens behind them, and fruit walls, which show here and there, among the nectarines, the vestiges of an old cloister arch or shaft, and looking in front on the cathedral square itself, laid out in rigid divisions of smooth grass and gravel walk, yet not uncheerful, especially on the sunny side, where the canons' children are walking with their nurserymaids. And so, taking care not to tread on the grass, we will go along the straight walk to the west front, and there stand for a time, looking up at its deep-pointed porches and the dark places between their pillars where there were statues once, and where the fragments, here and there, of a stately figure are still left, which has in it the likeness of a king, perhaps indeed a king on earth, perhaps a saintly king long ago in heaven, and so higher and higher up to the great mouldering wall of rugged sculpture and confused arcades, shattered, and grey, and grisly with heads of dragons and mocking fiends, worn by the rain and swirling winds into yet unseemlier shape, and coloured on their stony scales by the deep russet-orange lichen, melancholy gold; and so, higher still, to the bleak towers, so far above that the eye loses itself among the bosses of their traceries, though they are rude and strong, and only sees like a drift of eddying black points, now closing, now scattering, and now settling suddenly into invisible places among the bosses and flowers, the crowd of restless birds that fill the whole square with that strange clangour of theirs, so harsh and yet so soothing, like the cries of birds on a solitary coast between the cliffs and sea.

Think for a little while of that scene, and the meaning of all its small formalisms, mixed with its serene sublimity. Estimate its secluded, continuous, drowsy felicities, and its evidence of the sense and steady performance of such kind of duties as can be regulated by the cathedral clock; and weigh the influence of those dark towers on all who have passed through the lonely square at their feet for centuries, and on all who have seen them rising far away over the wooded plain, or catching on their square masses the last rays of the sunset, when the city at their feet was indicated only by the mist at the bend of the river.

JOHN RUSKIN, *The Stones of Venice*

If we duly weighed God's blessings we should see and feel that the greatest of all was in the ability to go to church: whether a cathedral, or the humblest of those grey turrets which are, to the Christian's eye, the most charming points of our English landscape – gems of sentiment for which our woods, and green slopes, and hedgerow elms are the lovely and appropriate setting.

SAMUEL PALMER

There is, perhaps, no greater hardship at present inflicted on mankind in civilized and free countries, than the necessity of listening to sermons. No one but a preaching clergyman has, in these realms, the power of compelling an audience to sit silent, and be tormented. No one but a preaching clergyman can revel in platitudes, truisms, and untruisms, and yet receive, as his undisputed privilege, the same respectful demeanour as though words of impassioned eloquence, or persuasive logic, fell from his lips. Let a professor of law or physic find his place in a lecture-room, and there pour forth jejune words and use-less empty phrases, and he will pour them forth to empty benches. Let a barrister attempt to talk without talking well, and he will talk but seldom. A judge's charge need be listened to perforce by none but the jury, prisoner, and gaoler. A

Member of Parliament can be coughed down or counted out. Town-councillors can be tabooed. But no one can rid himself of the preaching clergyman. He is the bore of the age, the old man whom we Sinbads cannot shake off, the nightmare that disturbs our Sunday's rest, the incubus that overloads our religion and makes God's service distasteful. We are not forced into church! No: but we desire more than that. We desire not to be forced to stay away. We desire, nay, we are resolute, to enjoy the comfort of public worship; but we desire also that we may do so without an amount of tedium which ordinary human nature cannot endure with patience; that we may be able to leave the house of God, without that anxious longing for escape, which is the common consequence of common sermons.

With what complacency will a young parson deduce false conclusions from misunderstood texts, and then threaten us with all the penalties of Hades if we neglect to comply with the injunctions he has given us! Yes, my too self-confident juvenile friend, I do believe in those mysteries which are so common in your mouth; I do believe in the unadulterated word which you hold there in your hand; but you must pardon me if, in some things, I doubt your interpretation. The Bible is good, the Prayer-book is good, nay, you yourself would be acceptable, if you would read to me some portion of those time-honoured discourses which our great divines have elaborated in the full maturity of their powers. But you must excuse me, my insufficient young lecturer, if I yawn over your imperfect sentences, your repeated phrases, your false pathos, your drawlings and denouncings, your humming and hawing, your ohing and ahing, your black gloves and your white handkerchief. To me, it all means nothing; and hours are too precious to be so wasted – if one could only avoid it.

And here I must make a protest against the pretence, so often put forward by the working clergy, that they are overburdened by the multitude of sermons to be preached. We are all too fond of our own voices, and a preacher is encouraged in the vanity of making his heard by the privilege of a compelled audience. His sermon is the pleasant morsel of his life, his delicious moment of self-exaltation. 'I have preached nine sermons this week,' said a young friend to me the other day, with hand languidly raised to his brow, the picture of an overburdened martyr. 'Nine this week, seven last week, four the week before. I have preached twenty-three sermons this month. It is really too much.' 'Too much, indeed,' said I, shuddering; 'too much for the strength of any one.' 'Yes,' he answered meekly, 'indeed it is; I am beginning to feel it painfully.' 'Would,' said I, 'you could feel it – would that you could be made to feel it.' But he never guessed that my heart was wrung for the poor listeners.

ANTHONY TROLLOPE, *Barchester Towers*

Dearest
. . . I went to church yesterday afternoon, according to pro-gramme – and saw and heard 'strange things upon *my* honour'!

The congregation consisted of some thirty or forty poor people – chiefly adults – who all looked at me with a degree of curiosity rather *'strong'* for the place. Reginald ascended the pulpit in his white *vestment*, and, in a loud, sonorous, perfectly Church-of-England-like tone, gave out the Psalm – whereupon there arose at the far end of the mouldering church, a shrill, clear sound, something between a squeal of agony and the highest tone of a bagpipe! I looked in astonishment, but could discover nothing – the congregation joined in with the invis-ible thing, which continued to assert its predominance – and it was not till the end of the service that Hesketh informed me the strange instrument was 'a clarionet'!! Necessity is the mother of invention!

The service went off quite respectably; it is wonderful how little faculty is needed for saying prayers *perfectly well*! But when we came to the sermon! – greater nonsense I have often enough listened to – for, in fact, the sermon (Mrs Buller with her usual sincerity informed me before I went) 'was none of *his*; he had scraped together as many written by other people as would serve him for years – *which was much better for the congregation'*, but he delivered it exactly as daft Mr Hamilton used to read the newspaper – with a noble disdain of everything in the nature of a *stop* – pausing just when he needed breath at the end of a sen-tence, or in the middle of a word, as it happened! In the midst of this extraordinary exhortation an infant screamed out, 'Away, mammy! Let's away!' and another bigger child went off in whooping cough! For my part, I was all the while in a state between laughing and crying – nay, doing both alternately.

There were two white marble tablets before me, containing, one, the virtues of a wife and the sorrow of her husband (Capel Loft), the other a beautiful character of a young girl dead of consumption – and both concluded with 'hopes of an immortality through Jesus Christ'. And there was an old sword and sword-belt hung on the tomb of another Loft – killed in Spain at the age of 28; he also was to be raised up thro Jesus Christ. And this was the Gospel of Christ I was hearing – made into something worse than the cawing of rooks. I was glad to get out, for my thoughts rose into my throat at last, as if they would choke me; and I privately vowed never to go there, when worship was going on again!

JANE CARLYLE, letter to her husband, 15 August 1842

Lines from a Parish Magazine

I am a loyal Anglican,
    A Rural Dean and Rector;
I keep a wife and pony-trap,
    I wear a chest-protector.
I should not like my name to be
    Connected with a party;
But still my type of service is
    Extremely bright and hearty.

Of course, one has to keep abreast
    Of changing times and manners;
A Harvest Festival we keep,
    With Special Psalms and banners;
A Flower-Service in July,
    A Toy-Fund Intercession,
And, when the hens lay well, we hope
    To start an Egg-Procession.

My wife and I composed a form
   For dedicating hassocks,
Which (slightly changed) we also use
   For surplices and cassocks;
Our Bishop, when we sent it for
   His Lordship's approbation,
Remarked: 'A very primitive
   And pleasing compilation.'

To pick the best from every school
   The object of my art is,
And steer a middle course between
   The two contending parties.
My own opinions would no doubt
   Be labelled 'High' by many;
But all know well I could not wish
   To give offence to any.

One ought, I'm certain, to produce
   By gradual education
A tone of deeper Churchmanship
   Throughout the population.
There are, I doubt not, even here
   Things to be done in plenty;
But still – you know the ancient saw –
   'Festina lentè – *lentè.*'

I humbly feel that my success,
   My power of attraction,
Is mainly due to following
   This golden rule of action:
'See us from all men's point of view,
   Use all men's eyes to see with,
And never preach what anyone
   Could ever disagree with.'

G. W. E. RUSSELL

A City of London Communion Service

It was a wonderful spring morning; the churchyard was filled with flowers and on the many benches people were sitting, letting the warm sun bathe their faces. Some of them were reading, some were eating sandwiches and feeding crumbs to sparrows, and others were just resting, content in the miracle of spring.

The churchyard was the more peaceful and quiet, because of the noise in the background of cars and buses. It was like a ballet set and I expected any moment that somebody would get up and do a *pas seul* and then suddenly the whole place would be filled with dancing figures.

I went into the church. It was a Palladian affair in the eighteenth-century style, very light and gay with various marbles. There were three people in the church, the priest, the verger and a young man.

I knelt and pretended to pray. There was no one to pray to, but I felt terribly sorry for the priest. Out there in his churchyard there were a hundred people glorying in the sunshine; and inside only the young man and the verger, who was paid to be there, and me. I didn't count, because I was there on business. But for his sake I could pretend. . . .

It was twenty-seven years since I had heard the Order for Holy Communion. I had forgotten the beauty of its language. As the still familiar words came back to me, spoken bravely by the priest, it occurred to me that it might all be nonsense, but it was a *magnificent* waste of time and it did not matter if there were only one or two people in the congregation, provided that the churches were open. The very fact that in this busy city where at the moment almost everybody was engrossed in commerce, there was this priest celebrating the Lord's Supper to a legitimate congregation of one was magnificent.

At that moment the door of the church opened and a young woman, good-looking and well-dressed, but clearly worried about something, came in and knelt down to pray.

I found myself struggling with the Gloria, 'Glory be to God on high, and in earth peace, good will towards men. We praise thee, we bless thee, we give thanks to thee for thy great glory, O Lord God, heavenly King, God the Father Almighty.' It was merely an exercise in memory, how much one could remember after all those years.

'O Lord, the only-begotten Son Jesu Christ; O Lord God, Lamb of God, Son of the Father, that takest away the sins of the world, have mercy upon us . . .' I couldn't go on, even for the priest's sake. The idea of Jesus Christ taking away the sins of the world was impossible.

I looked at the girl, who seemed absolutely engrossed in her prayer. The priest raised his hands in benediction. 'The peace of God which passeth all understanding, keep your hearts and minds in the knowledge and love of God, and of his Son Jesus Christ our Lord: and the blessing of God Almighty, the Father, the Son and the Holy Ghost, be amongst you and remain with you always.'

That was no good for me. 'But I hope it's some use to you,' I thought, 'because you're a jolly worried young woman.'

ARTHUR CALDER MARSHALL, *No Earthly Command*

I liked our chapel, which was tall and full of light, and yet still; and colour-washed pale green and blue, with a bit of lotus pattern. And over the organ-loft, 'O worship the Lord in the beauty of holiness,' in big letters.

That was a favourite hymn too:

> O worship the Lord, in the beauty of holiness,
>   Bow down before Him, His glory proclaim;
> With gold of obedience and incense of lowliness
>   Kneel and adore Him, the Lord is His name.

I don't know what the 'beauty of holiness' is, exactly. It easily becomes cant, or nonsense, but if you don't think about it – and why should you? – it has a magic. The same with the whole verse. It is rather bad, really, 'gold of obedience' and 'incense of lowliness'. But in me, to the music, it still produces a sense of splendour.

I am always glad we had the Bristol hymn-book, not Moody and Sankey. And I am glad our Scotch minister on the whole avoided sentimental messes such as 'Lead, Kindly Light', or even 'Abide With Me'. He had a healthy preference for healthy hymns.

> At even, ere the sun was set,
>   The sick, O Lord, around Thee lay,
> Oh, in what divers pains they met!
>   Oh, in what joy they went away!

And often we had 'Fight the good fight with all thy might'.

In Sunday School I am eternally grateful to old Mr Remington, with his round white beard and his ferocity. He made us sing! And he loved the martial hymns:

> Sound the battle-cry,
> See the foe is nigh.
> Raise the standard high
> For the Lord.

The ghastly sentimentalism that came like a leprosy over religion had not yet got hold of our colliery village. I remember when I was in Class II in the Sunday School, when I was about seven, a woman teacher trying to harrow us about the Crucifixion. And she kept saying: 'And aren't you sorry for Jesus? Aren't you sorry?' And most of the children wept. I believe I shed a crocodile tear or two, but very vivid is my memory of saying to myself: 'I don't *really* care a bit.' And I could never go back on it. I never *cared* about the Crucifixion, one way or another. Yet the *wonder* of it penetrated very deep in me.

Thirty-six years ago men, even Sunday School teachers, still believed in the fight for life and the fun of it. 'Hold the fort, for I am coming.' It was far, far, from any militarism or gun-fighting. But it was the battle-cry of a stout soul, and a fine thing too.

Stand up, stand up for Jesus,
Ye soldiers of the Lord.

Here is the clue to the ordinary Englishman – in the Nonconformist hymns.

D. H. LAWRENCE, 'Hymns in a Man's Life', *Selected Essays*

Why are the Clergy . . . ?

Why are the clergy of the Church of England
Always altering the words of the prayers in the Prayer Book?
Cranmer's touch was surer than theirs, do they not respect
   him?
For instance last night in church I heard
(I italicize the interpolation)
'The Lord bless you and keep you *and all who are dear unto you*'
As the blessing is a congregational blessing and meant to be
This is questionable on theological grounds
But is it not offensive to the ear and also ludicrous?
That 'unto' is a particularly ripe piece of idiocy
Oh how offensive it is. I suppose we shall have next
'Lighten our darkness we beseech thee oh Lord *and the darkness
   of all who are dear unto us*'
It seems a pity. Does Charity object to the objection?
Then I cry, and not for the first time to that smooth face
Charity, have pity.

STEVIE SMITH

Bournemouth

The long wood of Scotch firs twists down towards the shore
A narrow wood of firs, laurel and spruce. All round,
The town lies, masquerading as a village more,
Strewn in among the trees, red bungalows galore,
The whitewashed seaside villas on the lower ground.

A gloomy wood that starts high up against the sky
And zigzags down, digs dells, then climbs up inky-green
To fall again in spinneys, single trees awry
Where daylight gilds the graves, a sleepy cemetery
Of dappled terraces, cool, vague and dimly seen.

Down left, the heavy tower (still waiting for a spire)
Belonging to a church you cannot see from here
And far away, the beach. The tower like some proud squire:
The Church of England deigns to patronize the shire.
No heavenward yearning, no humility, no fear.

The weather that I love; one of those rare still days
With neither cloud nor sun. The sun seems to withhold
Itself. Dancing up there behind the clearing haze,
The turning firmament a cream rose-petal glaze
The atmosphere of pearl, the sea of faded gold.

The Protestants' high tower sings with the sound of bells
First two or three or four, then eight together as one.
Instinctive harmony, an echoing song that tells
Of joy and loud despair; reproaches and compels,
A golden, brazen voice, with red fire in its tone.

The sound so vast and pure; the long wood listening
Music is not so fine; the chime, the sweet delay
Making the sea air shake, vibrate and quake and sing
The way that men in step will make a roadway ring
With echoes of the war from half a mile away.

The clangour dies; a trail of crimson cloud burns down
Throbs sobbing out at sea; extinguished, is at rest.
The new year's sunset, cold as lightning, daubs the town
Blood-red. It waits, head bowed, as it receives a crown
Of gathering night, the light still brilliant in the west.

Dusk deepens, icy cold; the sea still frets and mauls
The groynes along the shore, gruff surf, dull undertow
Sucking the shingle back; black groaning wooden walls,
That bear the brutal beating, leaking waterfalls
Dull beating tedium I, poor sinner, used to know.

*   *   *

Oh loneliness of heart, and oh, soul's emptiness,
The winter winds at war, the sea's dark swell,
Pride conquered, grieved to death and groaning in distress,
Black night that beckons on to folly, filthiness;
Reeks of catastrophe, the anteroom of hell.

Then, suddenly, three bells. Three flute-notes sound, and cease.
Three more, and then three more! The Angelus that seemed
Forgotten has returned; it says 'Oh be at peace
The Word made Flesh has won thy soul's release
A Virgin is with child, the sinful world redeemed.'

So God speaks in the voice of His poor little shrine,
There, half way up the wood's edge, on the right hand side.
Oh Rome! Our Mother Church! The call, that touch divine
That brings me back content, 'spite this sad heart of mine,
With practical advice: behold Christ crucified!

The night is velvet-soft; drained at the falling tide
The shore grows slowly still, deserted by the flood.
A broad, straight open road I follow satisfied
The whole way home, consoled, walking with hastening stride
In utter blackness through the long and silent wood.

PAUL VERLAINE (trs. John Wells)

223

Elegy in a Country Churchyard

The men that worked for England
They have their graves at home:
And bees and birds of England
About the cross can roam.

But they that fought for England,
Following a falling star,
Alas, alas for England
They have their graves afar.

And they that rule in England,
In stately conclave met,
Alas, alas for England
They have no graves as yet.

G. K. CHESTERTON

EPILOGUE

I went up in gloom, by the nearest spur, on to the grass and into the loneliness of the high Downs that are my brothers and my repose; and, once upon their crest, setting my face eastward I walked on in a fever for many hours back towards the places from which we had come; and below me as I went was that good landscape in which I had passed such rare and memorable hours.

I still went on, through little spinnies here and there, and across the great wave tops and rolls of the hills, and as the day proceeded and the light declined about me I still went on, now dipping into the gaps where tracks and roads ran over the chain, now passing for a little space into tall and silent woods wherever these might stand. And all the while I came nearer and nearer to an appointed spot of which a memory had been fixed for years in my mind. But as I strode, with such a goal in view, an increasing loneliness oppressed me, and the air of loss and the echo of those profound thoughts which had filled the last words we four had exchanged together.

It was in the grove above Lavington, near the mounds where they say old kings are buried, that I, still following the crest of my hills, felt the full culmination of all the twenty tides of mutability which had thus run together to make a skerry in my soul. I saw and apprehended, as a man sees or touches a physical thing, that nothing of our sort remains, and that even before my county should cease to be itself I should have left it. I recognized that I was (and I confessed) in that attitude of the mind wherein men admit mortality; something had already passed from me – I mean that fresh and vigorous morning of the eyes wherein the beauty of this land had been reflected as in a tiny mirror of burnished silver. Youth was gone out apart; it was loved and regretted, and therefore no longer possessed.

Then, as I walked through this wood more slowly, pushing before me great billows of dead leaves, as the bows of a ship push the dark water before them, this side and that, when the wind blows full on the middle of the sail and the water answers loudly as the ship sails on, so I went till suddenly I remembered with the pang that catches men at the clang of bells what this time was in November; it was the Day of the Dead. All that day I had so moved and thought alone and fasting, and now the light was falling. I had consumed the day in that deep wandering on the heights alone, and now it was evening. Just at that moment of memory I looked up and saw that I was there. I had come upon that lawn which I had fixed for all these hours to be my goal.

It is the great platform just over Barl'ton, whence all the world lies out before one. Eastward into the night for fifty miles stretched on the wall of the Downs, and it stretched westward towards the coloured sky where a full but transfigured daylight still remained. Southward was the belt of the sea, very broad, as it is from these bare heights, and absolutely still; nor did any animal move in the brushwood near me to insult the majesty of that silence. Northward before me and far below swept the Weald.

The haze had gone; the sky was faint and wintry, but pure throughout its circle, and above the Channel hung largely the round of the moon, still pale, because the dark had not yet come.

But though she had been worshipped so often upon such evenings and from such a place, a greater thing now moved and took me from her, and turning round I looked north from the ridge of the steep escarpment over the plain to the rivers and the roofs of the Weald. I would have blessed them had I known some form of word or spell which might convey an active benediction, but as I knew none such, I repeated instead the list of their names to serve in place of a prayer.

The river Arun, a valley of sacred water; and Amberley Wild brook, which is lonely with reeds at evening; and Burton Great House, where I had spent nights in November; and Lavington also and Hidden Byworth; and Fittleworth next on, and

Egdean Side, all heath and air; and the lake and the pine trees at the mill; and Petworth, little town.

All the land which is knit in with our flesh, and yet in which a man cannot find an acre nor a wall of his own.

I knew as this affection urged me that verse alone would satisfy something at least of that irremediable desire. I lay down therefore at full length upon the short grass which the sheep also love, and taking out a little stump of pencil that I had, and tearing off the back of a letter, I held my words prepared.

My metre, which at first eluded me (though it had been with me in a way for many hours) was given me by these chance lines that came:

> '. . . and therefore even youth that dies
> May leave of right its legacies,'

I put my pencil upon the paper, doubtfully and drew little lines, considering my theme. But I would not long hesitate in this manner, for I knew that all creation must be chaos first, and then gestures in the void before it can cast out the completed thing. So I put down in fragments this line and that; and thinking first of how many children below me upon that large and fruitful floor were but entering what I must perforce abandon, I wrote down:

> '. . . and of mine opulence I leave
> To every Sussex girl and boy
> My lot in universal joy.'

Having written this down, I knew clearly what was in my mind.

The way in which our land and we mix up together and are part of the same thing sustained me, and led on the separate parts of my growing poem towards me; introducing them one by one; till at last I wrote down this further line:

> 'One with our random fields we grow.'

And since I could not for the moment fill in the middle of the verse, I wrote the end, which was already fashioned:

'. . . because of lineage and because
The soil and memories out of mind
Embranch and broaden all mankind.'

Ah! but if a man is part of and is rooted in one steadfast piece
of earth, which has nourished him and given him his being,
and if he can on his side lend it glory and do it service (I
thought), it will be a friend to him for ever, and he has out-
flanked Death in a way.

'And I shall pass' (thought I), 'but this shall stand
Almost as long as No-Man's Land.'

'No, certainly,' I answered to myself aloud, 'he does not die!'
Then from that phrase there ran the fugue, and my last stanzas
stood out clear at once, complete and full, and I wrote them
down as rapidly as writing can go.

'He does not die' (I wrote) 'that can bequeath
Some influence to the land he knows,
Or dares, persistent, interwreath
Love permanent with the wild hedgerows;
He does not die, but still remains
Substantiate with his darling plains.

'The spring's superb adventure calls
His dust athwart the woods to flame;
His boundary river's secret falls
Perpetuate and repeat his name.
He rides his loud October sky:
He does not die. He does not die.

'The beeches know the accustomed head
Which loved them, and a peopled air
Beneath their benediction spread
Comforts the silence everywhere;
For native ghosts return and these
Perfect the mystery in the trees.

'So, therefore, though myself be crosst
The shuddering of that dreadful day
When friend and fire and home are lost
And even children drawn away –
 The passer-by shall hear me still,
 A boy that sings on Duncton Hill.'

Full of these thoughts and greatly relieved by their metrical
expression, I went, through the gathering darkness, southward
across the Downs to my home.

HILAIRE BELLOC, *The Four Men*

ACKNOWLEDGEMENTS

We are grateful to the following authors, owners of copyright, publishers and literary agents who have kindly given permission for poems and passages of prose to appear in this anthology.

Antique (Winter 1986) for passage by Auberon Waugh.
Arthur Calder-Marshall for extract from *No Earthly Command* (1957).
Jonathan Cape Ltd for the poem 'The Bungalows' by William Plomer.
Century Hutchinson Publishing Group Ltd for the poem 'The Coast – Norfolk' by Frances Cornford, and the poem 'The Diehards' by Ruth Pitter.
Chatto & Windus Ltd, The Hogarth Press Ltd for extract from *London Perceived* by V. S. Pritchett.
Claud Cockburn for extract from *In Time of Trouble*.
Rosica Colin Ltd on behalf of the Richard Aldington estate, for the poem 'Eros and Psyche' by Richard Aldington.
William Collins Sons & Co. Ltd for extract from *The Collins Guide to Parish Churches* by John Betjeman.
André Deutsch Ltd for the poem 'England Expects' by Ogden Nash.
Dobson Books Ltd for material from *Round Trip (Letter to Henry Miller)* by Alfred Perles.
Gerald Duckworth & Co. Ltd for material from *Everyday England* by Monica Redlich and from *English Journey* by Beryl Bainbridge.
Faber & Faber Ltd for stanza from 'Bucolics' from *Collected Poems* by W. H. Auden; extract from *The Dog Beneath the Skin* by W. H. Auden and Christopher Isherwood; the poem 'Wessex Guidebook' from *The Collected Poems of Louis MacNeice*; the poem 'Cut Grass' from *High Windows* by Philip Larkin; and the poem 'Here' from *Whitsun Weddings* by Philip Larkin.
F. G. Ferguson Publishing Co. (USA) for extract from *The English People* by George Orwell.
The Folio Society Ltd for two extracts from a translation of *Voltaire's England* translated by Desmond Flower (1950).
Oliver D. Gogarty on behalf of the estate of Oliver St John Gogarty

for extract from *A Weekend in the Middle of the Week*.

Graham Greene for extracts from *The Lawless Roads*.

Hamish Hamilton Ltd for extract from *A Life with Alan* by Eva Taylor (1987).

Sir Rupert Hart-Davis and Mrs Eva Reichmann for extract from *Mainly on the Air* by Max Beerbohm; extract from *Going Back to School* by Max Beerbohm; and extract from 'A Letter from the Seaside' in *Electric Delights* by William Plomer.

A. M. Heath & Co. Ltd on behalf of the late Sonia Brownell Orwell's estate and Martin Secker & Warburg (Publishers), for extract from *Coming Up for Air* by George Orwell; and extract from *Evening Standard* (15.12.1945) in *Collected Journalism* by George Orwell.

A. M. Heath & Co. Ltd on behalf of the Patrick Hamilton estate, for material from *2000 Streets Under the Sky* by Patrick Hamilton.

David Higham Associates Ltd for extract from *Burke's Steerage* by T. H. White; extract from *England Have My Bones* by T. H. White; extract from *Quite Early One Morning* by Dylan Thomas.

Henry Holt & Co. (USA) for extract from *The Compleat Imbiber* by John Betjeman.

The Marvell Press for the poem 'Church Going' in *The Less Deceived* by Philip Larkin.

Professor J. P. Mayer for extract from *Journeys to England and Ireland* by Alexis de Tocqueville (London, 1958).

John Murray (Publishers) Ltd for extract from *Burne-Jones Talking* edited by Mary Lago (1981); the poem 'Business Girls' by John Betjeman; extract from the poem 'Beside the Seaside' by John Betjeman; extract from *First and Last Loves* by John Betjeman; and 'Lines from a Parish Magazine' from *A Londoner's Log Book* by G. W. E. Russell.

James MacGibbon on behalf of the Stevie Smith estate, for extract from the poem 'O Happy Dogs of England' and extract from the poem 'Why are the Clergy . . . ?' in *Collected Poems of Stevie Smith* (Penguin Modern Classics).

Macmillan Publishers Ltd for extract from *A Very Private Eye* by Barbara Pym (1984).

John O'Connor for extract from *Canals, Barges and People* (Art and Technics, 1950).

Oxford University Press for extract from 'Blockley, Gloucestershire' by William Trevor from *Places: An Anthology of Britain* chosen by Ronald Blythe (1981).

Peters, Fraser & Dunlop Group Ltd for extract from *The Four Men* by Hilaire Belloc.

Ms Frédérique Porretta for extract from *England* by Nikos Kazantzakis (1965).

Quartet Books Ltd for extract from *Winter Notes on Summer Impressions* by Fyodor Dostoyevsky translated by K. Fitzlyon (1985); for extract from *The Speakers* by Heathcote Williams (1964).
Queen for extract by William Trevor.
Sir James M. Richards for extract from *The Castles on the Ground*.
Routledge & Kegan Paul (Associated Book Publishers (UK) Ltd) for extracts from *Discoveries in England* by Emile Cammaerts (1930).
The Society of Authors and Mrs Nicolete Gray on behalf of the Laurence Binyon estate, for extract from the poem 'The Burning of the Leaves' by Laurence Binyon.
The Spectator for extract from *Homage to a Leader*, article by John Stewart Collis (*Spectator*, 30 January 1982).
Thames & Hudson Ltd for extract from *Notes on England* by Hippolyte Taine, translated by E. Hyams (1957).
Viking (Penguin Books) for extract from *Romney Marsh* illustrated and described by John Piper (1950).
Virago for extract from *Me Again* by Stevie Smith.
A. P. Watt Ltd for extract from *An Irishman's England* by John Stewart Collis; on behalf of Lady Hopkinson and Michael Holroyd, executors of the Robert Graves estate, for the poem '1805' from *Collected Poems* (1975) by Robert Graves; and on behalf of the executors of the Hesketh Pearson estate for material from *This Blessed Plot* (1942).
George Weidenfeld & Nicolson Ltd for extract from *Speak, Memory* by Vladimir Nabokov.

INDEX OF AUTHORS

INDEX OF SUBJECTS